Leading Mainframe Modernization with Agentic AI

Mainframes

Ricardo Nuqui

Published by Isaac Nangan, 2025.

Table of Contents

Leading Mainframe Modernization
with Agentic AI

Leading Mainframe Modernization with Agentic AI

A Practical Reference Guide for Enterprise Leaders, Architects, and Practitioners

Ricardo Nuqui

LEADING MAINFRAME MODERNIZATION WITH AGENTIC AI

Leading Mainframe Modernization with Agentic AI

First edition. December 2025.

Written by Ricardo Nuqui

To Coleen, Sky and Neo. You are my inspirations.

Preface

Mainframes continue to sit at the very heart of the world's most critical systems. From global banking and insurance platforms to government services, transportation networks, and large-scale retail operations, these systems process trillions of dollars in transactions every day with unmatched reliability, security, and performance. Yet despite their importance, many organizations still struggle with a familiar tension: how to modernize these environments without putting stability, compliance, or institutional knowledge at risk.

At the same time, Artificial Intelligence—particularly **Agentic AI**—is reshaping how work gets done across the enterprise. AI is no longer limited to passive analytics or isolated automation. It can now observe, decide, act, and learn within clearly defined boundaries. When applied thoughtfully, this new class of AI offers a powerful opportunity: not to replace the mainframe, but to *elevate it.*

This book was written to bridge that gap.

Why This Book Exists

Much of the conversation around AI and modernization assumes that legacy systems must be abandoned or replaced. In practice, that approach is often unrealistic, risky, and unnecessary. The mainframe is not the problem—outdated processes, limited visibility, and manual operational bottlenecks are.

Agentic AI provides a way forward. By embedding intelligent agents into existing workflows, organizations can enhance decision-making, reduce operational friction, and gradually modernize how mainframe systems are operated and managed—without rewriting decades of proven business logic.

This companion book exists to help you do exactly that.

Who This Book Is For

This book is written for:

- Mainframe professionals seeking practical, future-ready skills
- IT leaders responsible for modernization, resilience, and cost optimization
- Architects and engineers exploring AI-enabled operations
- Managers and executives who need to align AI initiatives with business outcomes

You do **not** need to be an AI expert to benefit from this book. Concepts are explained in clear, operational terms, always grounded in real-world enterprise scenarios.

How to Use This Companion Book

This book is designed to complement the online course *Agentic AI for Mainframes*, but it also stands on its own as a long-term reference.

You can:

- Read it alongside the course lessons for deeper context
- Use specific chapters as implementation guides during projects
- Revisit frameworks, checklists, and case studies when planning or scaling initiatives

While the structure generally follows the progression of the course—from foundational concepts to leadership, execution, and real-world case studies—it also includes additional insights, examples, and practical guidance that go beyond what is possible in a video-based format.

A Practical, Responsible Approach to AI

Throughout this book, you will notice a consistent emphasis on responsibility, governance, and human oversight. Agentic AI is powerful, but in mission-critical environments, power must always be balanced with control, transparency, and trust.

This is not a book about hype.

It is a book about **practical progress**.

A Final Word

Mainframe modernization is not a one-time project—it is an ongoing journey. Agentic AI is not a destination, but a capability that evolves over time as systems, teams, and organizations mature.

If this book helps you ask better questions, make more informed decisions, and take confident, incremental steps toward AI-enabled modernization, then it has served its purpose.

Welcome to that journey.

Prologue

The Quiet Evolution of the World's Most Critical Systems

Every second of every day, millions of transactions move silently through mainframe systems around the world. Credit card payments clear in milliseconds. Payrolls are processed on time. Airline seats are confirmed. Insurance claims are validated. Government benefits are distributed.

Most people never see these systems. And that is precisely the point.

Mainframes were designed to be invisible—to work flawlessly in the background while the business moves forward. For decades, they have delivered unmatched reliability, security, and scale. Yet in boardrooms and technology forums, they are often spoken about as if they were fragile relics, holding organizations back from innovation.

The truth is far more nuanced.

The challenge facing enterprises today is not whether mainframes still matter—they clearly do. The challenge is how to *evolve* the way these systems are operated, monitored, and extended in a world that now expects real-time insight, adaptive decision-making, and continuous optimization.

This is where Agentic AI enters the picture.

From Automation to Agency

Traditional automation has long been part of mainframe operations. Scripts restart jobs. Schedulers trigger workflows. Alerts notify operators when something goes wrong. These tools are useful—but they are reactive, rigid, and heavily dependent on human intervention.

Agentic AI represents a fundamental shift.

An agent does not simply follow instructions. It observes its environment, evaluates options, takes action within defined boundaries, and learns from outcomes. In practical terms, this means AI systems that can:

- Detect emerging performance bottlenecks before SLAs are breached
- Recommend or execute corrective actions during batch or online processing
- Optimize workflows dynamically based on system behavior and business priorities
- Reduce operational noise while increasing visibility and control

Importantly, this evolution does not require ripping out existing systems or rewriting core business logic. Agentic AI works *with* the mainframe, not against it.

A Familiar Problem, Seen Through a New Lens

If you have worked in enterprise IT long enough, you have likely experienced the same recurring challenges:

- Critical knowledge locked in the heads of a few senior experts
- Manual processes that exist "because they've always been done that way"
- Overnight batch windows that get tighter every year
- Increasing pressure to do more with the same—or fewer—resources

These are not failures of technology. They are signals that the operating model itself needs to evolve.

Agentic AI offers a way to capture institutional knowledge, reduce dependency on manual intervention, and introduce adaptive intelligence into environments where change must be deliberate and controlled.

Not a Revolution—A Responsible Progression

This book is not about replacing people with machines. It is about *augmenting* human expertise.

In mission-critical environments, trust is earned through transparency, predictability, and control. Agentic AI must be designed with clear guardrails, strong governance, and well-defined escalation paths. Humans remain accountable. AI becomes a capable assistant—one that works tirelessly, consistently, and at scale.

The organizations that succeed will not be the ones that adopt AI the fastest, but the ones that adopt it *wisely*.

What Lies Ahead

As you move through this book, you will explore:

- How Agentic AI fits naturally into mainframe ecosystems
- Where AI-driven agents deliver immediate operational value
- How to scale intelligently without compromising stability or compliance
- What successful modernization looks like in real enterprise environments

You will also encounter practical frameworks, real-world scenarios, and lessons learned from organizations that have already begun this journey.

The mainframe has always evolved quietly—without fanfare, without disruption. Agentic AI is simply the next chapter in that evolution.

And it is a chapter being written right now.

Part I: Foundations – Understanding the Shift

Introduction

Before tools, architectures, or implementation strategies can be discussed, one essential question must be addressed:

Why is change necessary at all—especially for systems that already work?

For decades, mainframes have delivered exactly what enterprises needed most: stability, security, and scale. They process the world's most valuable transactions with a level of reliability few platforms can match. In many organizations, the mainframe is not just another system—it is the system of record.

And yet, the environment surrounding these systems has changed dramatically.

Business leaders now expect real-time insights instead of next-day reports. Customers expect instant responses instead of queued requests. Regulatory requirements demand continuous monitoring rather than periodic audits. At the same time, skilled mainframe professionals are retiring, workloads are growing, and operational complexity continues to rise.

These pressures do not diminish the value of the mainframe—but they do challenge the traditional ways it is operated and managed.

This first part of the book establishes the foundation for everything that follows. It reframes modernization not as a threat to mainframes, but as a necessary evolution of how intelligence, automation, and decision-making are layered on top of them.

Why Foundations Matter

Modernization efforts often fail not because of technology, but because of misunderstanding:

- Modernization is confused with migration

- Automation is mistaken for intelligence
- AI is treated as a tool rather than a capability

Agentic AI forces us to rethink these assumptions.

Before introducing agents, feedback loops, or autonomous decision-making, we must clearly understand:

- What modernization really means in a mainframe context
- Why traditional automation is no longer sufficient
- How Agentic AI represents a progression—not a disruption

Part I is designed to align mental models, terminology, and expectations. It ensures that everyone—technical practitioners, architects, and decision-makers alike—starts from the same conceptual ground.

Chapter 1: Why Mainframe Modernization Still Matters

The first chapter challenges a persistent myth: that modernization is something mainframes must *defend against*.

In reality, modernization is not about abandoning proven systems. It is about ensuring that those systems remain relevant, adaptable, and sustainable in the face of changing business demands. This chapter explores:

- Why mainframes continue to underpin global commerce
- The real drivers behind modernization initiatives
- Common misconceptions that derail modernization efforts
- How modernization can strengthen—not weaken—core systems

Rather than focusing on replacement, the discussion centers on evolution: modern interfaces, smarter operations, and better alignment with business outcomes.

Chapter 2: From Automation to Agentic AI

Automation has long been a cornerstone of mainframe operations—but its limitations are becoming increasingly clear.

This chapter introduces the conceptual leap from rule-based automation to agent-based intelligence. It explains:

- The differences between scripts, workflows, AI-assisted tools, and agents
- Why reactive automation struggles in complex environments
- How Agentic AI introduces adaptability, context, and learning
- What "agency" actually means in controlled enterprise systems

Most importantly, the chapter positions Agentic AI not as a black box, but as a transparent, governable capability that fits naturally into mainframe operations.

Setting the Stage for What Comes Next

By the end of Part I, readers will have a shared understanding of:

- The forces driving change in enterprise computing
- The role of AI in enhancing—not replacing—mainframe systems
- Why Agentic AI is emerging now, and not earlier
- How modernization, intelligence, and governance must evolve together

With this foundation in place, the book can move confidently into architectures, implementation strategies, governance models, and real-world applications—grounded in clarity rather than hype.

Part I is not about *how fast* to modernize.

It is about *why modernization matters*, and *what kind of intelligence modern enterprises now require*.

The journey begins here.

Chapter 1: Why Mainframe Modernization Still Matters

Mainframes are often discussed in extremes. On one side, they are praised as unbreakable pillars of enterprise computing. On the other, they are dismissed as outdated relics that must eventually be replaced. Both views miss a more important truth:

Mainframes are not obsolete—but the way we operate and evolve them must change.

Modernization is not about questioning the value of the mainframe itself. It is about ensuring that this value continues to compound in a world that now demands speed, adaptability, intelligence, and continuous insight.

This chapter examines why mainframe modernization remains critical today, clears away common misconceptions about "legacy systems," and explains how AI—particularly Agentic AI—reshapes the modernization conversation entirely.

The Enduring Role of the Mainframe in Modern Enterprises

Despite decades of predictions about their demise, mainframes remain deeply embedded in global enterprise operations. Banks,s, insurance companies, governments, airlines, and retailers continue to rely on them to process the most critical workloads.

Why?

Because mainframes excel at what matters most:

- **Unmatched reliability** – near-zero downtime for mission-critical workloads
- **Extreme scalability** – handling millions of transactions per second
- **Strong security and isolation** – built-in controls trusted by regulators

- **Cost efficiency at scale** – especially for high-volume transaction processing

In many organizations, the mainframe is not just another platform—it is the **system of record**, holding decades of business logic, customer data, and compliance rules that cannot simply be recreated elsewhere.

What *has* changed is the environment around the mainframe:

- Business cycles move faster
- Customer expectations are real-time
- Compliance is continuous, not periodic
- Skilled personnel are harder to replace

These pressures do not reduce the importance of the mainframe—they increase it. Modernization, therefore, is not optional; it is how enterprises protect and extend their most valuable digital assets.

Myths vs. Realities of "Legacy Systems"

The word *legacy* is often used imprecisely, and sometimes unfairly. Let's separate myth from reality.

Myth 1: Legacy means outdated and fragile

Reality: Many mainframe systems are more stable and resilient than newer platforms. Their longevity is evidence of robustness, not weakness.

Myth 2: Legacy systems can't integrate with modern technologies

Reality: Mainframes support APIs, event streams, containers, Linux workloads, and hybrid cloud integrations. The limitation is usually organizational, not technical.

Myth 3: Legacy code has no future value

Reality: Decades of encoded business logic represent institutional knowledge that is extremely difficult—and risky—to replicate elsewhere.

Myth 4: Legacy equals high cost

Reality: For predictable, high-volume workloads, mainframes often remain more cost-effective than distributed alternatives once infrastructure, licensing, and operational overhead are fully considered.

Calling a system "legacy" does not make it obsolete. It simply means it has survived long enough to prove its value. Modernization should respect that value—not erase it.

Modernization vs. Replacement: Strategic Trade-Offs

One of the most critical decisions enterprises face is whether to modernize existing systems or replace them entirely. This is rarely a purely technical choice—it is a strategic one.

Replacement Strategies

Replacement typically involves migrating workloads off the mainframe to cloud-native or distributed platforms.

Potential benefits:

- Access to modern tooling ecosystems
- Easier talent recruitment
- Perceived architectural simplicity

Risks and costs:

- Rewriting complex business logic
- Data migration risks
- Operational instability
- Regulatory exposure
- Long timelines with uncertain ROI

Many large-scale replacement initiatives fail not because of poor engineering, but because the complexity of the existing system was underestimated.

Modernization Strategies

Modernization focuses on enhancing what already works while addressing current limitations.

Typical approaches include:

- API-enabling existing applications
- Automating operations and workflows
- Introducing AI-driven insights
- Improving observability and responsiveness
- Integrating with hybrid cloud architectures

Modernization accepts a fundamental truth: **the fastest path forward is often through what already exists.**

Where AI Changes the Modernization Equation

Traditional modernization efforts focus on interfaces, infrastructure, and automation. AI introduces a new dimension: **intelligence**.

Instead of simply making systems faster or more connected, AI enables systems to:

- Analyze patterns across workloads
- Predict issues before they occur
- Optimize resource usage dynamically
- Assist or automate decision-making

Agentic AI goes even further by introducing systems that can:

- Operate with defined autonomy
- Adapt based on outcomes
- Coordinate actions across tools and platforms

- Act within governance boundaries

This changes modernization from a static upgrade into a **living capability**.

For example:

- An AI agent can detect abnormal transaction patterns and trigger investigations automatically
- Another agent can adjust batch schedules based on system load and business priority
- Yet another can guide junior operators by surfacing expert-level recommendations in real time

With AI, modernization is no longer just about *keeping up*. It becomes about *operating smarter.*

Why Modernization Still Matters—Now More Than Ever

Mainframe modernization matters today because:

- The business environment is no longer predictable
- Operational complexity continues to increase
- Skilled human oversight is becoming scarcer
- Intelligence must scale faster than headcount

Modernization is not a rejection of the past. It is a commitment to the future.

By combining the proven strengths of the mainframe with AI-driven intelligence, enterprises can transform systems of record into systems of insight—without sacrificing trust, stability, or control.

This sets the stage for the next chapter, where we move from *why modernization matters* to *how intelligence itself is evolving*—from automation to Agentic AI.

Chapter 2: From Automation to Agentic AI

For decades, enterprises have sought ways to reduce manual effort, improve consistency, and increase operational efficiency. Automation has always been part of this story—but the nature of automation has changed dramatically over time.

What began as simple scripts has evolved into intelligent systems capable of observing, deciding, and acting. Understanding this evolution is essential before introducing Agentic AI into mission-critical environments like the mainframe.

This chapter traces that journey, explains what truly makes AI "agentic," and clarifies why mainframes—often assumed to be incompatible with modern AI—are, in fact, ideal candidates for agent-driven workflows.

The Evolution of Enterprise Automation

Enterprise automation did not leap directly to AI. It evolved in stages, each solving a specific class of problems while introducing new limitations.

Stage 1: Scripts – Task Automation

The earliest form of automation relied on scripts:

- JCL jobs
- Shell scripts
- REXX routines
- Cron-based schedulers

These scripts executed predefined steps in a fixed order. They were fast and reliable—but entirely blind.

Strengths:

- Simple to implement

- Predictable behavior

Limitations:

- No awareness of context
- No adaptability
- Failure meant manual intervention

Scripts could execute tasks, but they could not reason about outcomes.

Stage 2: Rules Engines – Conditional Logic

As systems grew more complex, rule-based engines emerged:

- If–then logic
- Threshold-based alerts
- Policy-driven execution

Rules engines allowed systems to respond differently under specific conditions, such as:

- Restarting a job if it failed once
- Escalating alerts after repeated errors
- Routing tasks based on priority

Strengths:

- Greater flexibility
- Encoded business logic

Limitations:

- Rules are static
- Complexity grows exponentially

- Maintenance becomes difficult

Rules engines still required humans to anticipate every scenario in advance.

Stage 3: AI Assistants – Intelligence Without Autonomy

AI assistants introduced machine learning and natural language capabilities into enterprise workflows. These systems could:

- Analyze logs
- Recommend actions
- Answer operational questions
- Summarize system health

Examples include chat-based operational assistants or anomaly detection tools.

Strengths:

- Pattern recognition at scale
- Faster insights
- Improved decision support

Limitations:

- No authority to act
- Human approval required for execution
- Intelligence remains passive

AI assistants inform humans—but they do not operate systems.

Stage 4: AI Agents – Intelligence With Purpose and Action

Agentic AI represents a fundamental shift.

An AI agent does not just analyze or recommend. It:

- Observes system state

- Forms goals
- Selects actions
- Executes within defined boundaries
- Learns from outcomes

This is where automation becomes **adaptive, contextual, and autonomous**.

What Makes AI "Agentic"

Not all AI systems are agents. The term *agentic* refers to a specific set of characteristics that distinguish agents from tools.

An AI system is considered **agentic** when it exhibits:

1. Goal Orientation

Agents are designed to achieve outcomes, not just perform tasks.

- Maintain system availability
- Optimize throughput
- Reduce operational risk

They work continuously toward these objectives.

---

2. Environmental Awareness

Agents monitor signals such as:

- System metrics
- Job status
- Transaction volumes
- Error rates
- Security events

This awareness allows them to adapt actions in real time.

---

3. Decision-Making Capability

Agents evaluate options rather than follow fixed paths.

- Retry or escalate?

- Delay or reroute?
- Notify humans or self-correct?

Decisions are guided by policies, constraints, and learned behavior.

4. Controlled Autonomy

Agents act independently—but never without limits.

- Actions are scoped
- Permissions are enforced
- Auditing is mandatory

This makes agentic systems suitable for regulated environments.

5. Feedback and Learning

Agents improve over time by:

- Learning which actions succeed
- Adjusting thresholds
- Refining responses

This learning loop is what differentiates agents from traditional automation.

Human-in-the-Loop vs. Human-on-the-Loop Models

Introducing autonomous behavior into enterprise systems raises a critical question:

Where do humans fit?

Human-in-the-Loop

In this model:

- AI recommends actions
- Humans approve execution
- Control is direct and immediate

Best suited for:

- Early adoption
- High-risk decisions
- Compliance-sensitive actions

Trade-off: Slower response times and limited scalability.

Human-on-the-Loop

In this model:

- AI acts autonomously
- Humans supervise outcomes
- Intervention occurs by exception

Best suited for:

- High-volume operations
- Well-defined policies
- Mature governance frameworks

This model allows systems to operate at machine speed while preserving accountability.

Most enterprises adopt a **hybrid approach**, gradually moving from in-the-loop to on-the-loop as trust and governance mature.

Why Mainframes Are Ideal Candidates for Agentic Workflows

At first glance, mainframes may seem like unlikely hosts for cutting-edge AI. In reality, they possess qualities that make them uniquely suited for agentic systems.

1. Predictable and Structured Environments

Mainframe workloads are:

- Highly standardized
- Well-documented
- Consistent over time

This predictability is ideal for training and governing agents.

---

2. Rich Operational Telemetry

Mainframes generate extensive data:

- SMF records
- System logs
- Job statistics
- Performance metrics

Agents thrive on data—and mainframes provide it in abundance.

---

3. Strong Governance and Security Models

Built-in controls support:

- Role-based access
- Auditing and traceability
- Policy enforcement

These are foundational requirements for safe autonomy.

---

4. High-Value, Repetitive Workloads

Mainframes run tasks that are:

- Mission-critical
- Repetitive
- Time-sensitive

Automating and optimizing these with agents delivers immediate ROI.

---

5. Hybrid Integration Capabilities

Modern mainframes integrate seamlessly with:

- Cloud platforms
- APIs
- Event-driven architectures

This allows agents to coordinate actions across the enterprise—not just within the mainframe.

From Tools to Teammates

The transition from automation to Agentic AI marks a shift in how enterprises think about systems.

AI agents are no longer tools that wait for instructions. They become:

- Digital operators
- Continuous optimizers
- Risk mitigators
- Force multipliers for human expertise

For mainframe environments, this evolution is not disruptive—it is complementary. It enhances what already works while addressing the operational realities of modern enterprises.

With this foundation in place, the next part of this book moves from theory to practice—exploring how Agentic AI architectures are designed, governed, and implemented safely in real-world mainframe environments.

Part II: Core Concepts of Agentic AI for Mainframes

From Understanding to Enablement

In Part I, we explored *why* mainframe modernization still matters and *how* automation has evolved into Agentic AI. We established that agentic systems are not science fiction, nor are they a wholesale replacement for existing enterprise controls. They are a logical next step—especially in environments where reliability, predictability, and governance are non-negotiable.

Part II shifts the focus from **why** to **how**.

Before organizations can design, deploy, or govern AI agents on the mainframe, they must develop a shared understanding of what *Agentic AI actually means* in this context—and what technical foundations make it possible. This part introduces the core concepts that will be referenced throughout the remainder of the book and the accompanying course.

Why Core Concepts Matter

Agentic AI is often discussed using cloud-native assumptions:

- Stateless microservices
- Ephemeral compute
- Unbounded experimentation

Mainframes operate differently. They are:

- Stateful
- Deterministic
- Deeply integrated into enterprise risk models

Without grounding Agentic AI in mainframe realities, organizations risk creating solutions that are either unsafe, impractical, or unsustainable. Part II ensures that every concept introduced is mapped directly to the operational, architectural, and governance characteristics of mainframe systems.

Chapter 3: Defining Agentic AI in a Mainframe Context

Agentic AI does not have a single universal definition. What qualifies as "agentic" in a consumer application may be entirely unacceptable in a regulated enterprise environment.

Chapter 3 establishes a **mainframe-specific definition of Agentic AI**, addressing questions such as:

- What autonomy is appropriate on a mainframe?
- Where must human oversight remain mandatory?
- How do agents coexist with existing automation and operational roles?
- What distinguishes a true agent from a sophisticated script or AI assistant?

This chapter introduces a shared vocabulary for discussing agents—clarifying roles, responsibilities, boundaries, and trust levels. It also reframes agents not as replacements for operators, but as *operational partners* designed to reduce cognitive load and increase system resilience.

Chapter 4: Data as the Fuel – Logs, Metrics, and Signals

No agent can operate intelligently without situational awareness. On the mainframe, that awareness already exists—it is embedded in decades of operational data.

Chapter 4 focuses on **data as the enabling foundation of Agentic AI**, exploring:

- System logs, metrics, and events as real-time signals
- Historical data as a source of behavioral learning
- The difference between raw data and actionable signals

- How existing mainframe telemetry can be repurposed for agent decision-making

Rather than introducing new data sources, this chapter shows how organizations can unlock the value of what they already collect—but often underutilize.

What This Part Prepares You For

By the end of Part II, readers will:

- Understand how Agentic AI must be defined and constrained in mainframe environments
- Recognize the critical role of operational data in enabling agent behavior
- Be prepared to design agent architectures grounded in real system signals
- Have a mental model that supports safe, auditable autonomy

These core concepts form the foundation for Part III, where we move into **designing, implementing, and governing agentic workflows** that can operate confidently within the most mission-critical systems in the enterprise.

Part II does not ask you to build yet—but it ensures that when you do, you build on solid ground.

Chapter 3: Defining Agentic AI in a Mainframe Context

Agentic AI is often described in broad, sometimes vague terms—autonomous systems, goal-oriented intelligence, or AI that can "act on its own." While these descriptions may work in experimental or consumer-facing environments, they are insufficient—and often dangerous—when applied to mainframe systems.

In a mainframe context, *Agentic AI must be precise, bounded, and accountable.*

This chapter defines what Agentic AI truly means for mainframes by breaking it down into **roles, autonomy levels, behavioral models, and architectural patterns** that respect the realities of enterprise computing. The goal is not to maximize autonomy, but to maximize **trust, reliability, and operational value**.

Agent Roles: Observer, Advisor, Executor, and Coordinator

One of the most effective ways to demystify Agentic AI is to think in terms of **roles**, not intelligence levels. On the mainframe, agents do not need to be general-purpose thinkers. They need to perform specific operational roles exceptionally well.

1. Observer Agents

Observer agents monitor systems without taking action.

Typical responsibilities include:

- Parsing system logs, SMF records, and job outputs
- Detecting anomalies or deviations from baselines
- Correlating events across subsystems

Observer agents are **read-only by design**. They introduce no operational risk and are often the first type of agent organizations deploy. Their value lies in reducing human effort spent on routine monitoring and pattern recognition.

2. Advisor Agents

Advisor agents go one step further by making recommendations. Examples include:

- Suggesting JCL changes to improve job performance
- Recommending corrective actions for recurring job failures
- Highlighting potential capacity issues before thresholds are breached

Advisor agents do **not execute actions directly**. Instead, they present insights to operators, system programmers, or change managers. This role aligns closely with *human-in-the-loop* operating models and is ideal for regulated environments.

3. Executor Agents

Executor agents are authorized to take predefined actions automatically.

Common use cases include:

- Restarting failed batch jobs under controlled conditions
- Applying known remediation steps for well-understood issues
- Adjusting scheduling priorities within approved limits

Executor agents require strict safeguards:

- Clearly defined action scopes
- Pre-approved playbooks
- Comprehensive logging and audit trails

On mainframes, executor agents are typically constrained to **low-risk, high-confidence scenarios.**

4. Coordinator Agents

Coordinator agents manage interactions between multiple agents or workflows.

Their responsibilities include:

- Orchestrating observer, advisor, and executor agents
- Managing escalation paths when uncertainty increases
- Ensuring actions follow enterprise policies and priorities

Coordinator agents are particularly valuable in complex environments where batch processing, online systems, and monitoring tools must work together cohesively.

Decision Boundaries and Autonomy Levels

Agentic AI is not an all-or-nothing proposition. Autonomy exists on a spectrum, and mainframes demand careful placement along that spectrum.

Defining Decision Boundaries

Decision boundaries specify:

- What an agent *can decide*
- What requires *human approval*
- What is *explicitly forbidden*

For example:

- An agent may analyze job logs freely
- It may recommend parameter changes
- It may only execute changes during approved windows

Clear boundaries prevent unintended behavior and simplify audits.

Autonomy Levels in Practice

A practical autonomy model for mainframes often includes:

1. **Observe Only** – No decisions, no actions

2. **Recommend** – Decisions without execution
3. **Execute with Approval** – Actions after human confirmation
4. **Execute Automatically** – Actions within strict constraints

Most organizations operate multiple autonomy levels simultaneously, depending on task criticality.

Event-Driven vs. Goal-Driven Agents

Another critical distinction in agent design is **how agents decide when to act.**

Event-Driven Agents

Event-driven agents respond to specific triggers such as:

- Job failures
- Threshold breaches
- Security alerts

They are:

- Predictable
- Easier to test
- Easier to audit

Event-driven models align naturally with mainframe operations, where system events are well-defined and heavily logged.

Goal-Driven Agents

Goal-driven agents work toward defined outcomes, such as:

- Minimizing batch window overruns
- Maintaining system performance targets
- Reducing recurring operational incidents

These agents continuously evaluate system state and adjust actions accordingly. While powerful, goal-driven agents require tighter governance and are typically introduced later in an organization's agentic maturity.

Common Architectural Patterns

Agentic AI on mainframes does not require radical architectural disruption. Instead, it builds on familiar enterprise patterns.

Pattern 1: Agent as an Overlay

Agents operate externally, consuming logs and metrics without modifying core systems. This is the safest and most common starting point.

Pattern 2: Agent with Controlled Integration

Agents interact with system tools (e.g., schedulers, monitoring systems) through APIs or command interfaces, governed by strict permissions.

Pattern 3: Hybrid Human–Agent Workflow

Agents handle detection and analysis, while humans retain decision authority. This pattern maximizes trust and accelerates adoption.

Pattern 4: Federated Agents

Multiple specialized agents collaborate under a coordinator, each with narrow responsibilities. This mirrors traditional mainframe role separation and enhances resilience.

Why This Definition Matters

Defining Agentic AI correctly is not an academic exercise. It determines:

- What risks you introduce
- What controls you must implement
- How quickly teams will trust the system

When Agentic AI is framed as **role-based, bounded, and auditable**, it becomes a natural extension of mainframe operations—not a threat to them.

In the next chapter, we turn to the foundation that enables all of this: **data**. Specifically, how logs, metrics, and operational signals—already abundant in mainframe environments—become the fuel that allows agents to observe, reason, and act intelligently.

Chapter 4: Data as the Fuel – Logs, Metrics, and Signals

Agentic AI systems do not begin with intelligence—they begin with **data**. No matter how advanced an agent's reasoning capabilities may be, its effectiveness is entirely dependent on the quality, timeliness, and structure of the information it receives. In mainframe environments, this is both a challenge and a major advantage.

Mainframes generate **some of the richest operational data in enterprise computing**. For decades, these systems have been meticulously instrumented for reliability, auditability, and performance. The problem is not the lack of data—it is making that data accessible, usable, and meaningful for AI agents.

This chapter explores the primary mainframe data sources, the realities of data quality in long-lived systems, the trade-offs between real-time and historical data, and the practical steps required to prepare mainframe data for agentic AI consumption.

SMF, RMF, SYSLOG, and Operational Data Sources

Mainframe environments produce multiple layers of data, each serving a different operational purpose. For agentic AI, understanding the role of each data source is critical.

System Management Facilities (SMF)

SMF records are the backbone of mainframe operational analytics. They capture detailed information about:

- Job execution and resource consumption
- Dataset access and I/O activity
- Security events and user actions

For AI agents, SMF data provides **behavioral context**—what happened, when it happened, and under what conditions. Its structured nature makes it ideal for both historical analysis and pattern detection.

Resource Measurement Facility (RMF)

RMF focuses on performance and capacity metrics, including:

- CPU utilization
- Memory usage
- Workload performance indicators

RMF data is especially valuable for agents tasked with performance optimization, capacity planning, or early detection of resource saturation.

SYSLOG and Console Messages

SYSLOG captures system messages, warnings, and operator interactions. While less structured than SMF or RMF, it provides **situational awareness**, often revealing early signs of issues before formal failures occur.

Natural language processing techniques allow AI agents to extract signals from SYSLOG that were previously only interpretable by experienced operators.

Additional Operational Sources

Other valuable inputs include:

- Scheduler logs (e.g., batch job dependencies and failures)
- Application logs from COBOL, PL/I, or Java workloads
- Change management and incident records

When correlated, these sources allow agents to understand not just *what* happened, but *why* it happened.

Data Quality Challenges in Legacy Environments

Despite their richness, mainframe data sources present unique quality challenges.

Common issues include:

- Inconsistent formats across subsystems
- Cryptic message codes and abbreviations
- Limited contextual metadata
- Historical data designed for humans, not machines

Additionally, decades of system evolution may result in:

- Unused or poorly documented fields
- Custom extensions with tribal knowledge dependencies

Agentic AI does not eliminate these challenges—it **exposes them**. Poor data quality leads to poor recommendations, undermining trust in the system.

Real-Time vs. Historical Data for AI Agents

Effective agentic systems rely on both real-time and historical data, each serving a distinct purpose.

Real-Time Data

Real-time data enables agents to:

- Detect anomalies as they occur
- Trigger immediate alerts or actions
- Support event-driven workflows

However, real-time streams require careful filtering to avoid noise and false positives.

Historical Data

Historical data provides:

- Baselines for normal behavior
- Training material for models
- Long-term trend analysis

For goal-driven agents, historical data is essential for understanding seasonal patterns, workload cycles, and recurring incidents.

Balancing Both

Most successful implementations combine real-time detection with historical context, allowing agents to act quickly without losing perspective.

Preparing Mainframe Data for AI Consumption

Preparing data for agentic AI does not mean rewriting core systems. It means **making data usable without disrupting stability**.

Key preparation steps include:

- Normalizing data formats across sources
- Enriching records with contextual metadata
- Translating codes and abbreviations into human-readable forms
- Implementing data pipelines that respect security and compliance requirements

Crucially, data preparation should preserve:

- Data lineage
- Audit trails
- Original record integrity

This ensures that AI-driven insights remain explainable and defensible—an absolute requirement in enterprise and regulated environments.

Why This Chapter Matters

Agentic AI succeeds or fails based on its data foundation. Mainframes already produce the signals agents need—but only if those signals are made accessible and intelligible.

By treating logs, metrics, and operational data as strategic assets rather than byproducts, organizations unlock the true potential of agentic workflows. With the right data preparation, agents become reliable partners in operations—not black boxes.

In the next part of the book, we move from concepts to design, exploring **architectures, tooling, and integration strategies** that turn these data streams into actionable intelligence.

Part III: Planning Modernization with AI (Leadership View)

Technology does not modernize organizations—**leadership does.**

By this point in the book, you understand why mainframes still matter, how agentic AI differs from traditional automation, and why data is the fuel that makes intelligent workflows possible. What remains is the most difficult—and most decisive—part of the journey: **planning**.

This section shifts the lens from systems to **strategy**, from tools to **outcomes**, and from experimentation to **organizational commitment**. Agentic AI for mainframes cannot succeed as a purely technical initiative. It requires intentional leadership, disciplined governance, and a clear understanding of how AI-enabled modernization serves business priorities.

Many modernization efforts fail not because of technology limitations, but because of unclear goals, fragmented ownership, or overly ambitious scopes. Leaders often attempt to modernize everything at once, underestimate organizational resistance, or treat AI as an isolated innovation rather than a capability that must be woven into enterprise operations.

Part III is designed to prevent those mistakes.

From "Can We?" to "Why Should We?"

Modernization planning begins with purpose. Before selecting platforms, models, or architectures, leaders must answer fundamental questions:

- What problems are we actually trying to solve?
- Which outcomes matter most to the business right now?
- Where can AI deliver measurable value without disrupting core stability?

Chapter 5 focuses on establishing modernization goals that are meaningful, measurable, and aligned with enterprise priorities—not abstract innovation targets.

Aligning People, Power, and Accountability

AI initiatives inevitably cut across organizational boundaries. Infrastructure teams, application owners, security, compliance, operations, and business stakeholders all have legitimate interests—and concerns.

Chapter 6 addresses stakeholder mapping and governance, helping leaders design decision structures that enable progress while maintaining trust, compliance, and operational control.

Winning Early Without Overreaching

One of the most effective ways to build momentum is through early wins—initiatives that are small enough to manage, yet significant enough to demonstrate value.

Chapter 7 explores how to scope AI initiatives strategically, focusing on high-impact, low-risk use cases that create confidence and justify further investment.

Why This Part Matters

Agentic AI changes not just how systems operate, but how decisions are made. Leaders who approach modernization with clarity, discipline, and realism position their organizations to move faster—with less risk and greater buy-in.

Part III equips you with the planning mindset required to turn AI from an experimental concept into a trusted enterprise capability. The chapters that follow provide practical guidance for defining goals, aligning stakeholders, and shaping initiatives that succeed in real-world mainframe environments—not just in strategy decks.

With the planning foundation in place, the next phases of modernization can proceed with confidence, credibility, and purpose.

Chapter 5: Establishing Modernization Goals That Matter

Modernization succeeds or fails long before the first line of code is written or the first AI model is deployed. It succeeds—or fails—at the moment leaders decide **why** they are modernizing in the first place.

In mainframe environments especially, vague or technology-driven goals often lead to stalled initiatives, frustrated teams, and skeptical executives. This chapter focuses on helping leaders define modernization goals that are **clear, defensible, measurable, and aligned with real business needs**, not just technological ambition.

Business-Driven vs. Technology-Driven Goals

One of the most common mistakes in modernization programs is starting with the technology instead of the outcome.

A **technology-driven goal** sounds like this:

- "Implement AI on the mainframe"
- "Adopt agentic workflows"
- "Modernize legacy operations"

These statements may be directionally correct, but they do not explain **why** the organization should invest time, money, or political capital.

A **business-driven goal**, by contrast, connects modernization to outcomes leadership already cares about:

- Reducing incident resolution time for critical batch failures
- Improving system availability during peak processing windows
- Reducing operational risk caused by shrinking mainframe expertise
- Increasing audit readiness and compliance confidence

Agentic AI becomes compelling when it is framed as an **enabler**, not the objective itself. The goal is not "AI adoption." The goal is **better decisions, faster responses, and safer operations**—with AI as the mechanism that makes those goals achievable.

A practical leadership test:

If you removed the words "AI" and "modernization" from your goal statement, would it still make sense to the business?

If the answer is no, the goal likely needs refinement.

Translating Operational Pain Points into AI Opportunities

Mainframe environments are rich with operational friction—much of it accepted as "normal" simply because it has existed for decades.

Common pain points include:

- Repeated manual analysis of SMF or RMF data during incidents
- Overreliance on a small number of senior operators or systems programmers
- Reactive firefighting instead of proactive optimization
- Long mean time to diagnose (MTTD) performance issues
- High effort required to prepare audit evidence or compliance reports

These pain points are not just technical inconveniences; they are **signals of opportunity**.

Agentic AI excels when it can:

- Observe patterns humans miss
- Correlate signals across time and systems
- Recommend or execute actions consistently
- Preserve institutional knowledge that would otherwise walk out the door

For example, instead of stating:

"We want to deploy AI-based monitoring"

A stronger goal would be:

"We want to reduce unplanned batch delays by enabling AI agents to detect abnormal workload patterns and alert operations before SLA breaches occur."

The pain point provides the context. AI provides the leverage.

Defining Success Beyond "Cost Savings"

Cost savings are often cited as the primary justification for modernization, but they are rarely the most persuasive—or sustainable—measure of success.

In regulated, mission-critical environments, **risk reduction and resilience** often matter more than raw cost reduction.

Meaningful success metrics may include:

- Reduced operational risk exposure
- Faster incident detection and resolution
- Improved consistency in decision-making
- Higher system availability or predictability
- Reduced dependency on scarce expert roles
- Improved audit outcomes and regulatory confidence

For example:

- An AI agent that prevents a single major outage may justify its existence for years.
- An agent that standardizes operational responses reduces human error—even if headcount remains unchanged.
- An agent that produces audit-ready reports automatically may save weeks of effort during regulatory reviews.

Leaders should ask:

What would failure look like if we did *nothing*?

Often, the answer reveals that the cost of inaction is far greater than the cost of modernization.

Goal-Setting Frameworks Tailored for Regulated Environments

Mainframe modernization does not happen in a vacuum. Financial institutions, governments, and large enterprises operate under strict regulatory, security, and governance constraints.

This reality requires goal-setting frameworks that balance innovation with control.

Effective goal frameworks in regulated environments typically:

1. **Define clear boundaries**
   - What decisions can AI recommend?
   - What decisions require human approval?
2. **Emphasize traceability**
   - Can AI actions be explained, logged, and audited?
3. **Prioritize safety over speed**
   - Incremental deployment is preferred over "big bang" change
4. **Align with existing governance**
   - Goals should complement—not bypass—risk, compliance, and change management processes

A practical approach is to structure goals across three layers:

- **Operational goals** (e.g., reduce incident response time)
- **Risk and compliance goals** (e.g., improve audit traceability)
- **Capability goals** (e.g., establish reusable agent frameworks)

This layered approach allows leadership to communicate modernization goals clearly to both executives and technical teams, while satisfying regulatory expectations.

Leadership Insight

Establishing modernization goals is not about predicting the future perfectly. It is about **creating alignment, focus, and accountability**.

Agentic AI gives organizations powerful new capabilities—but only when those capabilities are aimed at the right targets. Leaders who invest time in defining goals that truly matter set the stage for modernization efforts that deliver value, build trust, and sustain momentum.

In the next chapter, we will explore how to identify and align the stakeholders who must support these goals—and how governance structures can enable progress instead of slowing it down.

Chapter 6: Stakeholder Mapping and Governance

Even the most well-defined modernization goals will struggle to move forward without the right people aligned behind them. In mainframe environments—especially those enhanced with agentic AI—success depends less on technology and more on **coordination, trust, and clear accountability**.

This chapter focuses on how leaders can identify the right stakeholders, align often-competing priorities, and establish governance structures that allow AI-enabled modernization to progress safely and confidently.

Identifying Executive, IT, and Operational Stakeholders

Mainframe modernization with AI touches far more than the IT department. One of the most common reasons initiatives stall is that key stakeholders are either not involved early—or not involved at all.

At a minimum, stakeholders typically fall into three broad groups:

Executive stakeholders

These include CIOs, CTOs, COOs, and business unit leaders. Their concerns usually center on:

- Business risk and continuity
- Regulatory exposure
- Return on investment
- Organizational readiness

Executives rarely want to know how an AI agent works internally—but they deeply care about what it can *safely* do and how it affects enterprise outcomes.

IT leadership and architecture teams

This group includes enterprise architects, infrastructure leads, security architects, and platform owners. Their priorities often include:

- System stability and performance
- Integration with existing tooling
- Security controls and access boundaries
- Long-term maintainability

They are typically the bridge between executive intent and operational reality.

Operational stakeholders

These are the people closest to the mainframe day-to-day:

- Systems programmers
- Operators
- Capacity planners
- Performance analysts
- Incident responders

Operational teams are both the greatest beneficiaries of agentic AI—and often the most skeptical. Their buy-in is essential, because they will:

- Validate whether AI recommendations are useful
- Decide when to trust or override agent actions
- Surface real-world constraints that leadership may not see

A practical rule:

If an AI agent affects someone's daily workflow, that person is a stakeholder—whether they are formally invited or not.

Aligning Risk, Compliance, and Innovation Teams

AI-driven modernization often creates tension between teams with very different mandates.

- **Innovation teams** want speed, experimentation, and learning.

- **Risk and compliance teams** want predictability, control, and evidence.
- **Security teams** want strict access control and minimal attack surface.

When these groups operate in silos, modernization slows—or fails outright.

Effective leaders treat governance not as a barrier to innovation, but as an **enabler of safe progress**. Alignment improves when:

- Risk and compliance teams are involved early, not as final approvers
- AI use cases are framed in terms of risk reduction, not just efficiency
- Controls are designed *into* workflows, not bolted on afterward

For example, an AI agent that recommends configuration changes can be positioned as:

- A compliance-enhancing control (consistent analysis and documentation)
- A risk-reducing advisor (human approval required before execution)
- An operational accelerator (faster diagnosis with fewer errors)

When innovation is presented as a way to strengthen governance—not bypass it—resistance drops significantly.

Decision Rights and Accountability Models

Agentic AI introduces a new and often uncomfortable question:

Who is accountable when an AI-driven decision affects production?

This is why clear decision rights are non-negotiable.
Effective accountability models define:

- What decisions AI agents can **observe**
- What decisions they can **recommend**
- What decisions they can **execute**
- When and how humans intervene

Common models include:

- **Human-in-the-loop**: AI recommends; humans approve
- **Human-on-the-loop**: AI acts autonomously within limits; humans supervise
- **Human-out-of-the-loop (rare in mainframes)**: AI acts independently, typically only in low-risk scenarios

Accountability should always remain human-owned. AI does not "own" outcomes; teams do. Clear documentation of decision boundaries protects both the organization and the people operating within it.

A useful leadership principle:

Autonomy increases only as trust, observability, and control mature.

Governance Structures for AI-Enabled Mainframes

Traditional mainframe governance structures—change advisory boards, risk committees, audit processes—do not need to be replaced. They need to be **extended**.

Effective AI governance structures typically include:

- A cross-functional AI oversight group
- Clearly documented AI policies and standards
- Approval processes tailored for AI-driven changes

- Mandatory logging, traceability, and explainability requirements

Rather than creating entirely new bureaucracy, successful organizations adapt existing governance to:

- Recognize AI agents as operational actors
- Require transparency into AI behavior
- Ensure consistent review and continuous improvement

Importantly, governance should scale with maturity. Early pilots require tighter controls; mature deployments can allow greater autonomy—without sacrificing accountability.

Leadership Insight

Stakeholder alignment and governance are not "soft" activities—they are strategic enablers.

Agentic AI amplifies decision-making power. Without clear ownership, aligned incentives, and trusted governance, that power becomes a liability. With them, it becomes a competitive advantage.

In the next chapter, we will focus on how to scope AI initiatives deliberately—starting small, delivering early wins, and building momentum without overwhelming systems or teams.

Chapter 7: Scoping AI Initiatives for Early Wins

One of the fastest ways to lose confidence in AI-driven modernization is to start too big. Ambitious visions are important, but early success is built on **careful scoping, disciplined restraint, and visible wins.** In mainframe environments—where stability and trust are paramount—how you start often matters more than where you eventually want to go.

This chapter focuses on how leaders and technical teams can identify the *right* AI initiatives to begin with, avoid common missteps, and design modernization roadmaps that build momentum without introducing unnecessary risk.

Choosing the Right First Use Cases

Early AI initiatives should do one thing exceptionally well: **prove value without threatening system stability**.

The best first use cases share several characteristics:

- High operational friction or manual effort
- Clear and repeatable decision patterns
- Low to moderate risk if recommendations are wrong
- Easy-to-measure outcomes

Common examples in mainframe environments include:

- Analyzing SMF or RMF data to identify performance anomalies
- Recommending capacity adjustments based on historical trends
- Flagging configuration drift or policy deviations
- Assisting operators during incident triage

These use cases allow AI agents to demonstrate insight and speed while keeping humans firmly in control. Early success is not about full automation—it is about **earning trust**.

A helpful litmus test:

If a human can easily override the AI without negative consequences, the use case is a good candidate for an early win.

What Not to Automate First

Just because something *can* be automated does not mean it *should* be—especially at the beginning.

Avoid starting with:

- Mission-critical changes with no rollback path
- Financial or regulatory decisions with strict audit requirements
- Security-sensitive actions such as access provisioning
- Complex workflows that rely heavily on undocumented tribal knowledge

These areas demand a deep understanding of edge cases and context—something AI agents develop only over time.

A common mistake is attempting to replace human judgment too early. Early AI initiatives should **augment expertise**, not challenge it. When experienced staff feel supported rather than displaced, adoption accelerates.

Balancing Ambition with Operational Safety

Effective scoping is a balancing act between innovation and caution.

Leaders should explicitly define:

- What success looks like in the first 90 days
- Acceptable levels of AI autonomy
- Clear rollback and fail-safe mechanisms

- Who has authority to pause or disable AI agents

This approach reframes AI as a controlled experiment rather than a disruptive force. By setting boundaries upfront, teams can move faster *within* those boundaries.

Operational safety is not the enemy of progress—it is what makes sustainable progress possible in mainframe environments.

Creating Phased Modernization Roadmaps

Early wins should not exist in isolation. Each initiative should be part of a broader, phased roadmap that evolves over time.

A typical phased approach might include:

1. **Observation phase** – AI analyzes data and surfaces insights
2. **Advisory phase** – AI recommends actions with human approval
3. **Assisted execution phase** – AI executes low-risk actions under supervision
4. **Scaled autonomy phase** – AI operates independently within defined limits

This progression allows trust, governance, and technical maturity to grow together.

Well-designed roadmaps also help executives see that AI modernization is not a one-time project, but a **capability-building journey**.

Leadership Insight

Early wins are not about showcasing cutting-edge AI—they are about proving reliability, value, and safety in real operational contexts.

By choosing the right first use cases, resisting premature automation, and planning modernization in phases, organizations create a foundation strong enough to support more advanced agentic AI capabilities later.

In the next part of this book, we will move from planning to execution—exploring the technical foundations and architectural patterns that turn AI strategy into operational reality on the mainframe.

Part IV Introduction: Integrating AI into Enterprise Strategy

Modernizing the mainframe with agentic AI is not a purely technical exercise—it is a **strategic transformation** that touches business priorities, operating models, and long-term enterprise direction. While earlier sections of this book focused on understanding agentic AI and planning safe, high-impact initiatives, this part shifts the lens outward. Here, we explore how AI-enabled mainframes fit into the broader enterprise strategy.

Too many AI initiatives fail not because the technology does not work, but because they operate in isolation. When AI is treated as a side project rather than a strategic capability, it struggles to gain executive support, sustained funding, and organizational adoption. For mainframe environments—often central to revenue, risk, and regulatory compliance—misalignment between AI initiatives and business strategy can be especially costly.

Part IV focuses on **alignment**: aligning agentic AI with what the business is trying to achieve and ensuring it complements, rather than competes with, existing IT and hybrid cloud strategies.

From Operational Improvement to Strategic Advantage

Agentic AI can deliver immediate operational benefits—faster incident response, better capacity planning, reduced manual effort. But its true value emerges when these improvements support broader goals such as:

- Improving customer experience and service reliability
- Increasing organizational resilience and uptime
- Enabling faster product launches and system changes
- Reducing operational risk in regulated environments

In this part, we examine how leaders can translate technical AI capabilities into **business-relevant outcomes** that executives understand and support.

AI as a First-Class Citizen in Enterprise Architecture

Mainframes no longer exist in isolation. They operate alongside distributed systems, cloud platforms, SaaS applications, and data pipelines. Agentic AI must therefore be designed to work **across boundaries**, not reinforce silos.

This section also addresses a common misconception: that AI-driven modernization of the mainframe is at odds with cloud or hybrid strategies. In reality, agentic AI can become the connective tissue that improves visibility, coordination, and decision-making across the entire IT landscape.

What This Part Covers

- **Chapter 8: Aligning Agentic AI with Business Strategy**
  Explores how to connect AI initiatives to business goals, executive KPIs, and value narratives that resonate beyond IT.
- **Chapter 9: Integrating with IT and Hybrid Cloud Strategy**
  Examines how agentic AI fits into enterprise architecture, DevOps models, and hybrid environments—ensuring the mainframe remains a strategic asset rather than a technological island.

Together, these chapters help leaders and practitioners position agentic AI not as an experimental tool, but as a **core enabler of enterprise strategy**, ensuring that mainframe modernization delivers lasting business impact rather than short-term technical wins.

Chapter 8: Aligning Agentic AI with Business Strategy

Agentic AI delivers its greatest value when it is **deliberately aligned with what the business is trying to achieve**. Without this alignment, even the most technically impressive AI solutions risk becoming expensive experiments that fail to gain traction or long-term support. In mainframe environments—where systems are mission-critical and deeply embedded in business operations—strategic alignment is not optional; it is essential.

This chapter explores how to ensure that agentic AI initiatives support enterprise objectives, strengthen digital transformation efforts, and enhance organizational resilience—while avoiding the common trap of deploying AI simply because it is fashionable.

Connecting AI Initiatives to Enterprise OKRs

Most modern organizations use **Objectives and Key Results (OKRs)** or similar frameworks to translate strategy into measurable outcomes. Agentic AI initiatives should map clearly and directly to these goals.

From Technical Outcomes to Business Results

A common mistake is defining AI success in purely technical terms, such as:

- Reduction in manual tickets
- Faster log analysis
- Improved system alerts

While valuable, these outcomes must be translated into business language:

- Reduced service downtime affecting customers
- Faster recovery from revenue-impacting incidents

- Improved compliance reporting accuracy

Practical Mapping Example

Consider a financial institution with the following enterprise objective:

- **Objective:** Improve digital service availability for customers
- **Key Result:** Reduce critical system outages by 30%

An aligned agentic AI initiative might:

- Monitor SMF and system logs continuously
- Detect early signals of performance degradation
- Recommend or execute pre-approved corrective actions

In this case, the AI agent is not a technical novelty—it is a direct contributor to a measurable business outcome.

Supporting Digital Transformation Goals

Digital transformation is often misunderstood as cloud migration alone. In reality, it is about **improving speed, reliability, insight, and adaptability** across the enterprise—including the mainframe.

How Agentic AI Advances Transformation

Agentic AI supports digital transformation by:

- Reducing manual, reactive operations
- Enabling faster decision-making with real-time insights
- Improving cross-platform coordination between mainframe and distributed systems
- Allowing teams to focus on innovation instead of firefighting

For example, an AI agent that correlates mainframe batch delays with upstream application changes enables faster root-cause analysis across platforms—something traditional tools struggle to achieve.

Modernization Without Disruption

Importantly, agentic AI allows organizations to modernize **how** the mainframe is operated without replacing **what** it does. This preserves stability while introducing intelligence, making it an ideal modernization lever for risk-averse environments.

AI as an Enabler of Business Resilience

Resilience has become a board-level concern. Enterprises are expected to withstand:

- System failures
- Cyber incidents
- Sudden workload spikes
- Regulatory and audit pressures

Agentic AI strengthens resilience by moving operations from reactive to proactive.

Resilience in Practice

Agentic AI can:

- Detect abnormal patterns before outages occur
- Recommend throttling, workload redistribution, or failover actions
- Maintain detailed audit trails of decisions and actions
- Support human operators during high-pressure incidents

Rather than replacing people, AI agents act as **force multipliers**, helping teams respond faster and more consistently under stress.

Avoiding "AI for AI's Sake"

One of the biggest risks in enterprise AI adoption is pursuing AI initiatives without a clear problem to solve. This often results in:

- Overly complex solutions
- Poor adoption by operations teams

- Difficulty demonstrating ROI

Guiding Principles to Stay Grounded

To avoid this trap:

- Start with a clearly defined operational or business pain point
- Set strict decision boundaries for AI agents
- Require measurable outcomes tied to business metrics
- Pilot before scaling

If an AI agent cannot be clearly explained in terms of business value, it likely does not belong in a production mainframe environment—at least not yet.

Strategic Alignment as a Continuous Process

Alignment is not a one-time exercise. As business priorities evolve, AI workflows must adapt. Regular reviews between IT, operations, and business leadership help ensure that agentic AI remains relevant, trusted, and impactful.

When aligned correctly, agentic AI becomes more than an automation tool—it becomes a **strategic capability** that strengthens the enterprise, protects critical systems, and enables confident modernization of the mainframe.

Chapter 9: Integrating with IT and Hybrid Cloud Strategy

Agentic AI for mainframes does not operate in isolation. In modern enterprises, the mainframe is part of a **broader, interconnected ecosystem** that includes distributed systems, private clouds, public cloud services, and SaaS platforms. For agentic AI to deliver sustained value, it must be deliberately integrated into the organization's overall IT and hybrid cloud strategy.

This chapter focuses on how to align agentic AI-enabled mainframes with distributed and cloud environments, ensuring interoperability, scalability, and architectural coherence—without introducing unnecessary complexity or silos.

Mainframe + Distributed + Cloud Alignment

Most enterprises today run **hybrid environments by design**, not by accident. Core systems of record often remain on the mainframe, while systems of engagement, analytics, and innovation increasingly live on cloud and distributed platforms.

Defining Clear System Roles

A sound integration strategy begins by clarifying roles:

- **Mainframe:** System of record, transaction integrity, high-volume batch and online processing
- **Distributed systems:** Application logic, user interfaces, microservices
- **Cloud platforms:** Elastic compute, analytics, AI services, and experimentation

Agentic AI can act as a **coordination layer**, helping these environments work together more intelligently. For example, an AI agent may detect a batch delay on the mainframe and notify or trigger adjustments in downstream cloud-based applications that depend on that data.

Interoperability Considerations

Interoperability is the foundation of successful hybrid strategies. Without it, AI agents become trapped within technical boundaries, limiting their effectiveness.

Key Interoperability Challenges

Common challenges include:

- Proprietary data formats and protocols
- Latency between platforms
- Inconsistent monitoring and logging standards
- Security and identity mismatches

Agentic AI workflows must be designed with these realities in mind, ensuring that agents can:

- Access consistent, normalized data
- Communicate across platforms securely
- Correlate events from multiple environments

Designing for Cross-Platform Awareness

Effective AI agents understand context beyond the mainframe. For instance, a performance anomaly may originate in a cloud-hosted API but surface as a transaction slowdown on z/OS. Interoperability allows agents to see—and act on—the full picture.

API Enablement and Service Exposure

APIs are the primary mechanism for integrating mainframes into hybrid architectures. They transform monolithic capabilities into **consumable, reusable services.**

Why APIs Matter for Agentic AI

APIs allow AI agents to:

- Query system status and metrics
- Trigger approved operational actions
- Exchange insights with other agents or systems
- Participate in broader enterprise workflows

For example, a mainframe-based AI agent may expose a service that reports batch completion status, which is then consumed by a cloud-based orchestration tool.

Governed, Not Open-Ended

API enablement must be:

- Secure
- Version-controlled
- Auditable
- Aligned with enterprise integration standards

This ensures that AI-driven interactions enhance agility without increasing risk.

Avoiding Architectural Silos

One of the most common pitfalls in modernization initiatives is the creation of **new silos**—this time around AI.

How Silos Form

Silos often emerge when:

- AI solutions are developed independently by isolated teams
- Tools and platforms are chosen without enterprise alignment
- Knowledge and ownership are unclear

This can lead to duplicated efforts, inconsistent practices, and reduced trust in AI outcomes.

Breaking Down Barriers

To avoid this:

- Establish shared architectural principles for AI and integration
- Encourage cross-team collaboration between mainframe, cloud, and security teams
- Use common observability, governance, and reporting frameworks

Agentic AI should function as a **bridge**, not a barrier—connecting platforms, teams, and data into a cohesive operational ecosystem.

A Unified Strategy for Sustainable Modernization

When agentic AI is integrated into the broader IT and hybrid cloud strategy, it becomes a powerful enabler of modernization rather than a standalone experiment. It allows enterprises to:

- Preserve the strengths of the mainframe
- Leverage the flexibility of cloud platforms
- Operate complex systems with greater intelligence and confidence

By aligning architecture, integration, and governance, organizations can ensure that agentic AI supports long-term strategic goals—without sacrificing stability, security, or control.

Part V: Measuring Value and Communicating ROI

As organizations move from experimentation to operational use of agentic AI on the mainframe, a critical question inevitably arises: **Is it working—and how do we prove it?** Modernization initiatives, especially those involving AI, succeed or fail not only on technical merit, but on the ability to demonstrate clear, defensible value to business and executive stakeholders.

Part V shifts the focus from *building and integrating* agentic AI to *measuring, validating, and communicating its impact*. In regulated, mission-critical environments like mainframes, value cannot be vague or anecdotal. It must be quantified, contextualized, and aligned with enterprise priorities such as reliability, risk reduction, operational efficiency, and resilience.

This part addresses a common gap in AI initiatives: teams often deploy intelligent capabilities but struggle to explain **why they matter** in business terms. Agentic AI may reduce mean time to resolution, prevent outages, improve operator effectiveness, or stabilize workloads—but unless these improvements are translated into meaningful metrics and executive-level narratives, they remain invisible at decision-making tables.

Chapter 10 focuses on defining the *right* metrics for AI-driven modernization. Traditional IT metrics alone are insufficient. Leaders need a balanced view that combines operational performance, risk indicators, human workload impacts, and long-term capability gains. This chapter introduces practical approaches to selecting metrics that reflect both technical excellence and business relevance.

Chapter 11 then turns those measurements into compelling communication. Executives, boards, and regulators do not need low-level technical detail—they need clarity, confidence, and evidence of control. This chapter explores how to present AI results in ways that resonate with management, support continued investment, and reinforce trust in AI-assisted operations.

Together, these chapters help bridge the final—and often most challenging—gap in modernization journeys: transforming technical success into **organizational confidence and sustained support**.

Chapter 10: Defining Meaningful Metrics for AI Modernization

One of the fastest ways an AI modernization initiative can lose momentum is by failing to answer a simple executive question: **"How do we know this is actually better?"** In mainframe environments—where stability, predictability, and accountability are paramount—metrics are not optional. They are the language of trust.

Agentic AI introduces new capabilities, but it does not eliminate the need for traditional operational discipline. Instead, it expands *what* should be measured and *how* success is defined. This chapter focuses on building a practical, credible measurement framework that demonstrates value without oversimplifying the complexity of AI-assisted operations.

Operational KPIs: Proving Stability Comes First

Before productivity or innovation gains are discussed, modernization efforts must demonstrate that core operational performance is preserved—or improved. Operational KPIs provide this foundation.

Key metrics include:

- **Mean Time to Resolution (MTTR)**
  Agentic AI often reduces MTTR by accelerating diagnosis, suggesting corrective actions, or executing pre-approved fixes. Tracking MTTR before and after AI introduction is one of the clearest indicators of operational value.
- **System Availability and Reliability**
  Availability metrics help confirm that AI-assisted workflows do not introduce instability. Improvements may come from earlier detection of anomalies or more consistent response patterns.

- **Resource Utilization (CPU, I/O, Memory)**
  AI-driven optimization can smooth workload spikes, improve batch scheduling, or reduce unnecessary retries. These improvements should be visible in utilization trends rather than isolated snapshots.

Operational KPIs reassure stakeholders that AI is enhancing—not jeopardizing—the mission-critical nature of the mainframe.

Financial and Productivity Metrics: Translating Technical Gains into Business Value

Once operational stability is established, attention shifts to efficiency and cost impact. Financial and productivity metrics help bridge the gap between technical improvements and executive priorities.

Common metrics include:

- **Labor Efficiency and Effort Reduction**
  Measuring reductions in manual intervention, repetitive analysis, or after-hours support provides insight into how AI changes day-to-day work—not just system performance.
- **Cost Avoidance vs. Cost Reduction**
  Many AI benefits come from *avoiding* incidents rather than cutting budgets outright. Prevented outages, reduced SLA penalties, and deferred infrastructure upgrades are all valid financial outcomes.
- **Throughput and Cycle Time Improvements**
  Faster batch completion, reduced job reruns, or quicker problem resolution translate directly into improved service delivery for downstream business processes.

The goal is not to force AI benefits into simplistic ROI formulas, but to present a credible picture of economic impact grounded in operational reality.

Risk Reduction and Compliance Indicators: Measuring What Didn't Go Wrong

In regulated environments, success is often defined by incidents that never occur. Agentic AI can play a significant role in risk mitigation, but these benefits must be measured intentionally.

Important indicators include:

- **Reduction in High-Severity Incidents**
  Fewer critical failures or production outages demonstrate that AI is improving early detection and response quality.
- **Policy and Control Adherence**
  Tracking how often AI actions align with predefined rules, approval workflows, and access controls reinforces governance confidence.
- **Audit Readiness and Evidence Quality**
  Improved logging, clearer decision traces, and consistent responses strengthen audit outcomes—even when AI is involved.

These metrics help shift the narrative from "AI as a risk" to "AI as a risk management tool."

Leading vs. Lagging Indicators: Measuring Today to Protect Tomorrow

A mature measurement framework balances **lagging indicators** (what already happened) with **leading indicators** (signals of what may happen next).

- **Lagging Indicators**
  MTTR reductions, cost savings, and incident counts confirm

past performance and are essential for reporting.

- **Leading Indicators**
  Early anomaly detection rates, AI recommendation accuracy, and operator override frequency provide insight into future reliability and adoption health.

Leading indicators are especially valuable in agentic systems, where early warning signals allow teams to adjust behavior before failures occur.

Building a Measurement System That Evolves

Metrics for AI modernization should not be static. As autonomy levels increase and trust grows, measurement frameworks must evolve to reflect new responsibilities and outcomes.

Effective teams:

- Start with a small, defensible metric set
- Align metrics to business and risk priorities
- Review and refine measurements as AI capabilities mature

By defining meaningful metrics early and revisiting them often, organizations create a shared understanding of success—one that supports both innovation and operational confidence.

In the next chapter, we move from measurement to communication: **how to present these results to management in ways that drive understanding, trust, and continued investment.**

Chapter 11: Presenting Results to Management

Even the most successful AI-enabled modernization effort can stall if its results are not communicated effectively. Executives rarely question the *potential* of AI—but they are highly sensitive to unclear value, unmanaged risk, and overly technical explanations. For Agentic AI initiatives on the mainframe, success depends not only on performance improvements, but on how those improvements are framed, contextualized, and justified.

This chapter focuses on turning metrics and outcomes into messages that resonate with senior leadership and decision-makers.

Translating Technical Gains into Executive Language

Technical teams often report success using system-level improvements: reduced job runtimes, fewer alerts, or faster root-cause analysis. While accurate, these metrics must be translated into outcomes executives care about.

Effective translation focuses on:

- **Business impact over system behavior**
  Instead of "MTTR reduced by 30%," communicate "production disruptions are resolved faster, protecting revenue and customer commitments."
- **Risk reduction over feature enhancement**
  Emphasize how AI lowers the likelihood of outages, compliance issues, or operational surprises.
- **Predictability and resilience**
  Highlight improved consistency, fewer escalations, and better preparedness for peak workloads or unexpected events.

Executives do not need to understand how the agent works—they need to understand why it matters.

Building Compelling ROI Narratives

ROI for Agentic AI is rarely a single number. It is a narrative that connects multiple dimensions of value into a coherent story.

Strong ROI narratives typically include:

1. **The original problem**
   Describe the operational pain point, risk exposure, or inefficiency that existed before AI was introduced.
2. **The intervention**
   Explain, at a high level, what changed—without technical jargon.
3. **The outcome**
   Present measurable improvements supported by data.
4. **The implication**
   Clarify what this means for the business moving forward: scalability, cost avoidance, or strategic flexibility.

This structure helps management see AI as a disciplined investment rather than an experimental technology.

Dashboards vs. Storytelling

Dashboards are essential—but they are not enough.

- **Dashboards**
  Provide ongoing visibility into KPIs, trends, and operational health. They support governance, monitoring, and accountability.
- **Storytelling**
  Provides context, meaning, and strategic insight. It explains *why* the numbers changed and *why that change matters now*.

The most effective presentations combine both:

- Dashboards for evidence
- Narratives for understanding and decision-making

Agentic AI initiatives benefit especially from storytelling, as autonomy and learning behavior are easier to trust when framed within real operational scenarios.

Common Mistakes When Reporting AI Success

Many AI initiatives struggle not because they fail—but because they are misunderstood. Common pitfalls include:

- **Overloading executives with technical detail**
  This creates confusion rather than confidence.
- **Overpromising future capabilities**
  Unrealistic expectations damage credibility when AI behaves conservatively—as it should in regulated environments.
- **Ignoring risk and governance discussions**
  Avoiding these topics raises red flags rather than reassurance.
- **Focusing only on short-term wins**
  AI modernization is a journey. Results should be positioned as cumulative progress, not isolated victories.

Clear, honest, and outcome-driven communication builds long-term executive trust.

Positioning AI as a Strategic Capability

When presented effectively, Agentic AI is no longer seen as a tool or experiment—it becomes a strategic capability embedded in enterprise operations. Management begins to ask better questions:

- Where else can this approach reduce risk?
- How can autonomy be expanded safely?

- What organizational changes are needed to scale success?

These are the conversations that signal true modernization.

With this chapter, we conclude **Part V: Measuring Value and Communicating ROI**—a critical bridge between technical execution and sustained leadership support. In the next part of the journey, we turn our attention to **operating, governing, and evolving Agentic AI in real-world mainframe environments**, where long-term success is truly defined.

Part VI: Change Management and Team Adoption

Technology alone does not modernize an organization—people do. While Agentic AI can transform how mainframe environments are monitored, optimized, and operated, its true impact depends on how well it is understood, trusted, and adopted by the teams who work with it every day.

Part VI focuses on the human side of AI-driven mainframe modernization. This is where many technically sound initiatives succeed or fail. Resistance, uncertainty, skill gaps, and cultural inertia can quietly undermine even the most advanced AI capabilities if they are not addressed deliberately. Conversely, organizations that invest in thoughtful change management often see AI adoption accelerate beyond initial expectations.

This section shifts the conversation from *what AI can do* to *how people work with AI*.

Why Change Management Matters More with Agentic AI

Agentic AI introduces a new operating model. Unlike traditional automation, AI agents:

- Observe and interpret system behavior
- Make recommendations or decisions
- Act with varying degrees of autonomy
- Learn over time

For operations teams, this represents a fundamental shift in responsibility, control, and trust. Long-standing mental models—where humans manually intervene at every step—must evolve toward supervision, exception handling, and strategic oversight.

Without intentional change management, teams may:

- Disable or bypass AI agents
- Over-rely on AI without understanding its limits
- Resist adoption out of fear of job displacement or loss of expertise

Part VI addresses these realities directly.

From Technical Enablement to Human Enablement

Earlier parts of this book focused on architecture, data, strategy, and measurement. This part recognizes that modernization is incomplete unless people are enabled alongside systems.

You will explore:

- How AI changes roles, workflows, and decision-making authority
- Why psychological safety and transparency are essential for trust
- How leaders can position AI as a partner, not a replacement
- What successful adoption looks like in real operational environments

The goal is not just acceptance of AI, but confident, effective collaboration between humans and intelligent systems.

What This Part Covers

Chapter 12: Human Factors in AI-Driven Modernization

Examines the emotional, cognitive, and organizational dynamics introduced by AI. This chapter explores trust, accountability, skill evolution, and the shifting identity of mainframe professionals in an AI-augmented world.

Chapter 13: Driving Adoption of AI Workflows

Focuses on practical strategies for embedding AI into daily operations. Topics include training approaches, phased rollouts, feedback loops, and leadership behaviors that reinforce adoption rather than resistance.

Preparing for Sustainable Modernization

Modernization is not a one-time deployment—it is an ongoing transformation. By addressing change management and team adoption explicitly, organizations create the conditions for Agentic AI to evolve safely and productively over time.

Part VI equips leaders, architects, and operations managers with the insights needed to ensure that AI-driven mainframe modernization is not only technically successful, but human-centered, resilient, and sustainable.

Chapter 12: Human Factors in AI-Driven Modernization

Mainframe modernization with Agentic AI is often discussed as a technical evolution—but in practice, it is just as much a human transformation. This chapter focuses on the people side of AI-driven change: the fears, expectations, habits, and cultural dynamics that determine whether AI becomes a trusted partner or an underused tool.

In mission-critical environments, where downtime is unacceptable and errors are costly, human factors carry even greater weight. Understanding and addressing these factors early is essential for sustainable modernization.

Resistance to AI in Mission-Critical Systems

Resistance to AI in mainframe environments is not irrational—it is often rooted in experience.

Mainframe professionals are trained to value:

- Predictability over experimentation
- Proven processes over untested innovation
- Manual control over opaque automation

When AI agents are introduced, especially those that recommend or execute actions, teams may perceive them as risky or unreliable simply because they are unfamiliar.

Common sources of resistance include:

- **Loss of control:** "If the AI makes the decision, what is my role?"
- **Opacity:** "I don't understand how the AI arrived at this recommendation."
- **Fear of failure:** "If something goes wrong, who is

accountable?"

Effective leaders acknowledge these concerns openly rather than dismissing them. Resistance often fades when teams see AI introduced gradually—starting with observation and advisory roles before moving toward execution.

A practical approach is to begin with **read-only or recommendation-only agents**. For example, an AI agent might analyze SMF data and suggest workload rebalancing actions without executing them. Over time, as recommendations prove reliable, trust naturally increases.

Addressing Job Security Concerns

One of the most sensitive issues in AI adoption is fear of job displacement.

In mainframe environments, this fear can be particularly acute. Many professionals have spent decades developing deep system knowledge and may worry that AI diminishes the value of their expertise.

Leaders must proactively reframe the narrative:

- AI does not replace expertise—it amplifies it
- AI handles repetitive analysis so humans can focus on judgment
- Domain knowledge becomes more valuable, not less

Concrete examples help:

- Instead of manually scanning logs, operators validate AI-identified anomalies
- Instead of reacting to incidents, teams focus on prevention and optimization
- Senior staff shift from "firefighting" to mentoring and governance roles

Organizations that successfully adopt Agentic AI often pair it with **upskilling initiatives**, helping teams learn how to supervise, tune, and interpret AI agents. This turns anxiety into opportunity.

Building Trust in AI Recommendations

Trust is not granted—it is earned.

For AI agents operating in mission-critical systems, trust grows through:

1. **Transparency:** Clear explanations of what data was used and why a recommendation was made
2. **Consistency:** Repeated, reliable performance over time
3. **Human oversight:** Clear escalation paths when humans disagree with AI output

For example, an AI agent recommending capacity adjustments should show:

- The metrics it analyzed
- The thresholds it detected
- Historical patterns that informed the recommendation

When teams can trace recommendations back to familiar operational data, AI feels less like a black box and more like an intelligent colleague.

Leaders should also normalize disagreement with AI. Encouraging teams to challenge recommendations—and learn from those discussions—strengthens trust rather than undermining it.

Psychological Safety and Experimentation

Agentic AI thrives in environments that allow learning, iteration, and refinement. However, many mainframe cultures are risk-averse by necessity.

Psychological safety bridges this gap.

Psychological safety means:

- Teams can experiment without fear of blame
- Mistakes are treated as learning opportunities
- Feedback is encouraged, not punished

Practical ways to foster this include:

- Running AI pilots in non-production or shadow modes
- Conducting post-incident reviews that include AI behavior analysis
- Celebrating lessons learned, not just flawless outcomes

When teams feel safe to experiment, they engage more deeply with AI systems and contribute insights that improve agent behavior over time.

The Leadership Imperative

Human factors do not resolve themselves—they require leadership attention.

Leaders set the tone by:

- Communicating clearly and consistently about AI's role
- Modeling trust in AI while maintaining accountability
- Investing in people as much as technology

In AI-driven modernization, success is not defined solely by system performance, but by how confidently and effectively humans collaborate with intelligent systems.

In the next chapter, we move from mindset to action—exploring how organizations can **drive adoption of AI workflows** and embed Agentic AI into everyday mainframe operations in a way that sticks.

Chapter 13: Driving Adoption of AI Workflows

Adopting Agentic AI on the mainframe is not a single deployment event—it is a behavioral shift. Even the most capable AI agents will fail to deliver value if they remain outside daily workflows or are treated as optional tools. This chapter focuses on how organizations move from *AI-enabled* to *AI-embedded*, where agents become a natural, trusted part of how work gets done.

Successful adoption happens when people clearly understand **how AI fits into their roles**, **how to work with it day to day**, and **how their feedback improves it over time**.

Training Models for Mixed-Skill Teams

Mainframe teams are rarely homogeneous. A single operations group may include:

- Veteran system programmers with decades of experience
- Mid-career engineers comfortable with automation
- Younger staff with AI or cloud exposure but limited mainframe depth

A one-size-fits-all training approach will not work.

Effective AI adoption uses **layered training models**, such as:

- **Foundational training** for all roles: what Agentic AI is, what it is not, and how it supports mission-critical systems
- **Role-based training** tailored to operators, system programmers, architects, and managers
- **Scenario-based learning** using real operational situations rather than abstract AI concepts

For example:

- Operators learn how to interpret AI alerts and recommendations
- System programmers learn how agents interact with SMF, RMF, and automation tools
- Managers learn how to read AI-driven dashboards and risk indicators

The goal is not to turn everyone into an AI expert—but to make everyone *AI-literate* within their role.

Redefining Roles and Responsibilities

Agentic AI changes *how* work is done, which means roles must evolve accordingly.

Without clear role redefinition, teams may:

- Duplicate AI efforts manually
- Ignore AI insights
- Assume someone else is responsible for AI outcomes

Organizations that succeed explicitly redefine responsibilities, such as:

- **Operators** become supervisors of AI-driven actions rather than manual executors
- **System programmers** act as AI governors, tuning thresholds and decision boundaries
- **Leads and managers** focus on exception handling, prioritization, and strategic optimization

A helpful mental model is:

AI handles detection and analysis; humans handle judgment and accountability.

This clarity reduces friction and ensures AI is seen as a collaborator—not a competitor.

Embedding AI into Daily Operations

AI adoption accelerates when agents are embedded directly into existing workflows rather than added as separate tools.

This means:

- AI insights appear in familiar dashboards
- Recommendations integrate with existing ticketing and incident systems
- AI outputs align with established operational processes

For example:

- An AI agent flags a performance anomaly and automatically opens a ticket with supporting evidence
- Capacity planning agents feed recommendations into weekly operations reviews
- Change management meetings include AI-generated risk assessments

When AI becomes part of *how work already happens*, adoption becomes natural rather than forced.

Creating Feedback Loops Between Humans and Agents

Agentic AI improves through interaction. Feedback loops are the mechanism that transforms static AI into continuously learning systems.

Effective feedback loops include:

- Allowing humans to approve, reject, or modify AI recommendations
- Capturing reasons for overrides or escalations
- Periodically reviewing AI decisions during post-incident or operations reviews

For example, when an operator overrides an AI recommendation, the system records:

- The context
- The alternative action taken
- The eventual outcome

Over time, these signals refine agent behavior and increase alignment with real-world operational judgment.

Equally important is *closing the loop* with humans—showing teams how their feedback improved AI performance. This reinforces engagement and ownership.

From Adoption to Ownership

The ultimate goal is not mere usage, but ownership.

When teams:

- Trust AI recommendations
- Understand how agents operate
- Actively shape agent behavior

AI workflows stop being "new technology" and become part of the organization's operational DNA.

Driving adoption requires patience, clarity, and leadership—but when done well, it unlocks the full potential of Agentic AI on the mainframe, enabling safer, smarter, and more resilient modernization.

With this foundation in place, organizations are no longer just modernizing systems—they are modernizing how humans and intelligent agents work together to run the enterprise.

Part VII: Real-World Case Studies and Patterns

Up to this point, this book has focused on *principles, frameworks, and strategies* for applying Agentic AI to mainframe modernization. But theory alone does not create confidence. Confidence comes from seeing how these ideas work in the real world—under real constraints, real risks, and real organizational dynamics.

Part VII bridges strategy and execution by examining how enterprises have actually applied Agentic AI to modernize their mainframe environments. Rather than focusing on individual tools or vendor-specific implementations, this section looks for *patterns*—repeatable approaches, decision paths, and organizational behaviors that consistently lead to success.

These case studies are not presented as perfect success stories. They include trade-offs, missteps, course corrections, and lessons learned. In regulated, mission-critical environments, modernization is rarely linear. What matters is not avoiding mistakes entirely, but recognizing them early and adapting intelligently.

Why Patterns Matter More Than Examples

Every organization's mainframe environment is unique. Workloads, regulations, staffing models, and technical debt differ widely across industries and regions. This makes direct imitation risky.

Patterns, on the other hand, are transferable.

By focusing on patterns, this part of the book helps you:

- Recognize common modernization starting points
- Understand which AI use cases tend to succeed first
- Identify organizational conditions that enable or block progress
- Apply lessons without copying architectures blindly

These patterns provide a practical lens for leaders and practitioners who want to move forward with confidence rather than experimentation alone.

Chapter 14: Case Study Patterns in Successful Modernization

Chapter 14 examines recurring patterns observed across multiple successful modernization initiatives. These patterns include:

- How organizations sequence AI adoption
- Where they introduce autonomy versus human oversight
- How governance evolves as trust in AI grows
- Why early wins often focus on observability, risk reduction, and decision support

Instead of highlighting one-off success stories, this chapter distills what *consistently works*—and why.

Chapter 15: Industry-Specific Use Cases

While patterns are transferable, context still matters. Chapter 15 explores how different industries apply Agentic AI based on their specific operational and regulatory realities.

You will see how:

- Financial institutions prioritize risk, compliance, and availability
- Government and public sector organizations balance modernization with policy constraints
- Retail and logistics environments focus on scale, throughput, and cost optimization
- Healthcare and insurance systems emphasize reliability, auditability, and trust

These use cases help you map general principles to your own industry, accelerating adoption while avoiding costly misalignment.

What You Will Gain from This Section

By the end of Part VII, you will be able to:

- Identify which modernization patterns fit your environment
- Anticipate challenges before they become blockers
- Communicate modernization ideas using real-world precedents
- Make informed decisions grounded in proven practice

This final section reinforces a central message of this book: **Agentic AI for mainframes is not experimental—it is already working.** The organizations that succeed are those that learn from others, adapt thoughtfully, and apply intelligence with discipline.

With these real-world insights, you are better equipped to turn strategy into sustained modernization impact.

Chapter 14: Case Study Patterns in Successful Modernization

Modernizing mainframe environments with Agentic AI is rarely about a single breakthrough moment. Instead, success tends to emerge from a series of deliberate, well-sequenced decisions made under real operational pressure. When examining successful modernization efforts across industries, clear patterns begin to surface—patterns that can guide leaders and practitioners toward safer, more effective outcomes.

This chapter distills those patterns by looking at *where organizations start, how successful teams behave, the pace of change they choose, and what can be learned from initiatives that did not deliver the expected results.*

Common Starting Points Across Industries

Despite differences in size, regulation, and business focus, most successful modernization efforts begin in remarkably similar places. Organizations rarely start by giving AI full control over mission-critical workloads. Instead, they focus on areas where visibility and decision support create immediate value with minimal risk.

Common starting points include:

- **Operational monitoring and anomaly detection**, using AI agents to observe SMF, RMF, and log data and surface unusual patterns
- **Incident triage and root-cause analysis**, where agents assist human operators by correlating events across systems
- **Capacity planning and performance optimization**, especially in environments with recurring workload spikes
- **Knowledge augmentation**, such as AI-driven runbooks or advisory agents that support less-experienced staff

These use cases succeed because they improve *situational awareness* before attempting automation. Organizations that start here build trust in AI while strengthening operational discipline.

What Successful Teams Did Differently

Technology alone does not explain success. The most effective modernization teams share several behavioral and organizational traits that set them apart.

Successful teams:

- **Defined clear decision boundaries** for AI agents from day one, explicitly stating what the agent could recommend versus what it could execute
- **Embedded domain experts into AI design**, ensuring models reflected real operational nuance rather than abstract assumptions
- **Measured progress early and often**, using operational metrics rather than waiting for financial ROI
- **Treated AI as a teammate**, not a replacement, reinforcing human-in-the-loop and human-on-the-loop models

Perhaps most importantly, successful teams invested time in *operational readiness*—updating processes, documentation, and escalation paths to accommodate AI-driven insights.

Incremental vs. Transformative Approaches

Modernization efforts generally fall along a spectrum between incremental improvement and transformative change.

Incremental approaches focus on:

- Adding intelligence to existing workflows
- Improving reliability, speed, and consistency
- Reducing cognitive load on operations staff

These initiatives tend to succeed quickly and build momentum. **Transformative approaches**, by contrast, aim to:

- Redesign workflows around agent coordination
- Introduce autonomous remediation
- Re-architect operational decision-making

While transformative efforts can deliver significant long-term gains, organizations that attempt them too early often encounter resistance, governance gaps, or operational risk. Case studies show that the most successful transformations *start incrementally* and evolve naturally as trust and capability grow.

Lessons Learned from Failed Attempts

Not all modernization initiatives succeed, and failed attempts offer some of the most valuable insights.

Common failure patterns include:

- **Over-automation too early**, where AI agents were given execution authority without sufficient observability or safeguards
- **Lack of stakeholder alignment**, particularly with risk, compliance, or operations teams
- **Poor data readiness**, leading to unreliable recommendations and loss of trust
- **Treating AI as a side project**, disconnected from core operational goals

In many cases, these initiatives did not fail because AI was ineffective—but because organizational readiness lagged behind technical ambition.

Key Takeaway

The most successful modernization efforts share a disciplined, pattern-driven approach: start with visibility, respect operational reality, evolve autonomy gradually, and learn continuously. By recognizing these patterns—and avoiding the traps exposed by failed initiatives—organizations can modernize their mainframe environments with confidence, safety, and lasting impact.

In the next chapter, we will look at how these patterns play out across specific industries, revealing how Agentic AI is adapted to distinct regulatory, operational, and business contexts.

Chapter 15: Industry-Specific Use Cases

While the core principles of Agentic AI for mainframes remain consistent, the way those principles are applied varies significantly by industry. Regulatory pressure, transaction volumes, risk tolerance, and operational maturity all shape how organizations design and deploy agentic workflows. In this chapter, we explore how different industries are applying Agentic AI to modernize mainframe environments—highlighting practical use cases that reflect real-world constraints and priorities.

Banking and Financial Services

Banks and financial institutions are among the most mature mainframe users—and also among the most cautious adopters of AI. Reliability, security, and regulatory compliance are non-negotiable, which makes agentic approaches particularly valuable when designed with strict governance.

Common use cases include:

- **Intelligent transaction monitoring**, where AI agents observe transaction flows and flag anomalies for fraud or operational issues without interrupting processing
- **Automated incident correlation**, linking payment failures, batch delays, and system alerts across platforms to accelerate root-cause analysis
- **Capacity and workload optimization**, especially during peak periods such as payroll runs, end-of-month processing, or market volatility
- **Change impact analysis**, using AI agents to predict downstream effects of configuration or application changes before deployment

In these environments, AI agents typically operate in advisory or coordinator roles first, reinforcing human oversight while improving speed and accuracy.

Insurance and Government Systems

Insurance providers and government agencies often manage complex, long-lived systems that evolve slowly but must remain continuously available. Agentic AI helps bridge the gap between aging applications and modern operational expectations.

Typical use cases include:

- **Claims and case-processing optimization**, where AI agents identify processing bottlenecks or unusual delays
- **Batch job reliability monitoring**, especially for overnight or end-of-cycle workloads
- **Policy and rule analysis**, assisting teams in understanding how decades-old logic impacts current operations
- **Operational knowledge preservation**, capturing institutional expertise as senior staff retire

In government systems, transparency and explainability are especially critical. AI agents are designed to justify recommendations clearly, supporting auditability and public accountability.

Retail, Logistics, and Utilities

Industries driven by volume and variability benefit from Agentic AI's ability to respond dynamically to changing conditions. Mainframes in these sectors often handle massive transaction loads tied directly to customer experience.

Representative use cases include:

- **Demand-driven workload scaling**, where agents anticipate transaction spikes during promotions, weather events, or seasonal cycles

- **Supply chain visibility**, correlating mainframe data with distributed systems to detect disruptions early
- **Outage prevention and recovery**, particularly for utilities where downtime has immediate public impact
- **Energy and resource optimization**, using AI-driven insights to reduce waste and improve efficiency

Here, agentic workflows often evolve faster toward semi-autonomous execution, especially in non-financial, non-regulated processes.

Highly Regulated Environments

Across all industries, highly regulated environments share a common set of constraints that shape AI adoption. Whether in healthcare, defense, or critical infrastructure, agentic systems must operate within tightly controlled boundaries.

Key characteristics include:

- **Strict governance frameworks**, defining what agents can observe, recommend, or execute
- **Comprehensive logging and audit trails**, ensuring every AI action is traceable
- **Human-on-the-loop oversight**, where humans retain veto authority over high-impact decisions
- **Gradual expansion of autonomy**, based on demonstrated reliability and compliance

In these settings, Agentic AI becomes less about speed alone and more about *consistency, defensibility, and risk reduction*.

Closing Perspective

Industry-specific use cases show that there is no one-size-fits-all approach to Agentic AI for mainframes. Success comes from aligning agent roles, autonomy levels, and governance models with industry realities. Organizations that respect these differences—and design accordingly—unlock modernization paths that are both innovative and safe.

With this chapter, we conclude the companion book's core exploration of Agentic AI for mainframes. The next step is yours: applying these patterns, principles, and use cases to your own environment, one carefully chosen initiative at a time.

Part VIII: Advanced Topics and Practical Guidance

As organizations move from experimentation to sustained, enterprise-wide use of Agentic AI on the mainframe, the conversation inevitably shifts. The question is no longer *"Can we do this?"* but *"How do we do this safely, responsibly, and at scale?"* Part VIII is where strategy meets operational reality—where advanced concepts are translated into concrete, defensible practices that stand up to scrutiny from auditors, regulators, security teams, and executive leadership.

By this stage of the journey, readers should already understand what Agentic AI is, how it integrates with mainframe environments, and how it delivers measurable value. What remains is the hardest part: ensuring that intelligent agents operate within clearly defined boundaries, protect mission-critical systems, and behave predictably even under stress, failure, or uncertainty. This is where many promising AI initiatives either mature—or stall.

Part VIII focuses on the guardrails that make Agentic AI sustainable over the long term. It addresses the risks unique to AI-enabled mainframes, including unintended decision cascades, security exposure, compliance drift, and over-automation. Just as importantly, it provides practical guidance on designing agent autonomy in a way that enhances human control rather than undermining it.

What This Part Covers

This part consists of two closely related chapters:

- **Chapter 16: Risk Management, Security, and Compliance**
  This chapter explores how to identify, assess, and mitigate risks introduced by AI agents operating in mission-critical environments. It covers security considerations, regulatory

expectations, auditability, and how to align AI behavior with existing enterprise risk frameworks—without slowing innovation to a halt.

- **Chapter 17: Designing Safe Agent Autonomy**
  This chapter dives into the mechanics of autonomy itself: how much freedom an agent should have, where decision boundaries should be drawn, and how to implement safeguards such as escalation paths, kill switches, and human oversight. It emphasizes designing agents that are powerful but predictable, adaptive but controlled.

Why This Part Matters

Advanced AI capabilities amplify both strengths and weaknesses. In a mainframe context—where systems underpin revenue, safety, and public trust—there is little tolerance for ambiguity or uncontrolled behavior. The guidance in this part helps ensure that Agentic AI becomes a trusted operational partner rather than a source of new risk.

Think of Part VIII as your practical playbook for responsible scale. It is designed for leaders, architects, and practitioners who are ready to move beyond pilots and into production-grade, enterprise-ready Agentic AI—without compromising the stability and integrity that mainframes are known for.

Chapter 16: Risk Management, Security, and Compliance

When Agentic AI enters the mainframe environment, it doesn't just introduce new capabilities—it introduces new responsibilities. Mainframes are trusted precisely because they are predictable, auditable, and secure. Any AI-enabled modernization effort that weakens those traits will quickly lose executive, regulatory, and operational support. This chapter focuses on how to manage risk without paralyzing innovation, ensuring that Agentic AI strengthens—rather than compromises—the core principles that make mainframes indispensable.

The goal is not to "make AI safe" in the abstract, but to make it **governable** in real-world enterprise conditions.

AI Governance in Mainframe Environments

AI governance is often misunderstood as a purely policy-driven exercise. In reality, effective governance combines **organizational controls, technical guardrails, and operational discipline**. In mainframe environments, governance must align with long-established practices such as change management, separation of duties, and formal approval workflows.

Key governance principles for Agentic AI on mainframes include:

- **Clear ownership**
  Every AI agent must have a defined business owner, technical owner, and risk owner. If an agent makes a recommendation or executes an action, it should always be clear who is accountable for its behavior.
- **Defined decision boundaries**
  Governance starts with deciding what an agent *can* and *cannot* do. For example:

- Observe and analyze system metrics autonomously
- Recommend actions to operators
- Execute predefined actions only under strict conditions
- Escalate to humans for high-impact decisions

- **Alignment with existing governance bodies**
  AI governance should integrate with existing IT governance, risk committees, and architecture review boards—not operate as a parallel structure. This reduces friction and increases acceptance.

A practical example:

In a financial institution, an AI agent analyzing SMF data may be governed under the same change advisory board (CAB) rules as performance tuning changes. The difference is that approvals define *agent behavior rules*, not one-time configuration changes.

Auditability and Explainability

Auditability is non-negotiable in mainframe environments. If an AI agent influences operations, its actions must be **traceable, reviewable, and explainable**—not just to data scientists, but to auditors and compliance officers.

Effective auditability requires:

- **Comprehensive logging**
  Every agent action should generate logs that answer:
    - What input data was used?
    - What decision was made?
    - What rule, model, or threshold triggered it?
    - What action was taken (or recommended)?
    - Was human approval involved?
- **Explainable decision paths**
  While deep learning models may be complex, agent decisions

should be wrapped in explainable logic layers. For example:

  - "CPU utilization exceeded threshold X for Y minutes"
  - "Historical pattern matched known incident class"
  - "Recommended action based on approved runbook"

- **Replay and review capability**
  Auditors should be able to reconstruct events after the fact—just as they do with batch jobs or system changes today.

A real-world scenario:

During a regulatory audit, an institution is asked why a batch workload was deprioritized during month-end processing. With proper auditability, the organization can show that an AI agent followed predefined rules, used approved metrics, and escalated the decision to an operator who confirmed the action.

Data Privacy and Access Controls

AI agents are only as trustworthy as the data they can access. In mainframe environments, this data often includes highly sensitive information—financial records, personal data, or government information. Strong access controls are essential to prevent AI agents from becoming unintentional data exposure risks.

Best practices include:

- **Principle of least privilege**
  Agents should only access the data they absolutely need. An agent monitoring system health does not need access to customer records.
- **Role-based and context-aware access**
  Agent permissions should mirror human roles:
  - Read-only access for monitoring agents
  - Limited write access for execution agents

    - Time-bound or condition-based permissions
- **Data masking and abstraction**
  Where possible, agents should work with aggregated, anonymized, or tokenized data rather than raw sensitive records.

Example in practice:

An AI agent optimizing workload scheduling may consume CPU, I/O, and queue metrics without ever seeing application payloads or customer identifiers—significantly reducing privacy risk.

Regulatory Considerations

Regulators are increasingly attentive to AI usage, especially in critical infrastructure and financial systems. While regulations vary by industry and geography, common expectations are emerging.

Organizations should be prepared to demonstrate:

- **Human oversight**
  Regulators expect humans to retain ultimate control, especially for high-impact decisions.
- **Documented controls and policies**
  This includes AI usage policies, escalation procedures, and incident response plans involving AI agents.
- **Model and rule governance**
  Changes to AI behavior should follow formal approval and testing processes, just like code changes.
- **Risk assessments and impact analysis**
  Before deploying an AI agent, organizations should assess:
    - Operational risk
    - Security risk
    - Compliance risk
    - Reputational risk

In highly regulated environments, a phased approach is often most effective—starting with advisory agents, progressing to limited execution, and expanding autonomy only after governance confidence is established.

Bringing It All Together

Risk management, security, and compliance are not obstacles to Agentic AI—they are **enablers of trust**. When governance is clear, auditability is strong, access is controlled, and regulatory expectations are met, organizations gain the confidence to scale AI beyond pilots and into core operations.

In the next chapter, we build on this foundation by addressing one of the most critical design challenges of all: **how much autonomy is safe, and how to design AI agents that act decisively without acting recklessly**.

Chapter 17: Designing Safe Agent Autonomy

Agentic AI delivers its greatest value when it is allowed to act—not just observe or advise. At the same time, autonomy in mission-critical mainframe environments must be earned, constrained, and continuously validated. The purpose of this chapter is to show how organizations can design **safe, progressive autonomy** for AI agents—maximizing benefits while preserving control, trust, and resilience.

Safe autonomy is not about limiting AI; it is about **designing intelligence with intent**.

Guardrails for Agent Behavior

Guardrails define the "operating envelope" within which an AI agent is allowed to function. In mainframe environments, these guardrails must be explicit, enforceable, and aligned with operational policies that have evolved over decades.

Effective guardrails include:

- **Policy-based constraints**
  Agent actions should be governed by formal policies, such as:
  - Approved runbooks
  - Change windows
  - Risk thresholds (CPU, I/O, batch impact)
  - Regulatory restrictions
- **Scope and boundary definitions**
  Agents should be limited by:
  - System scope (which LPARs, workloads, or applications)
  - Time scope (business hours vs. off-hours)
  - Action scope (recommend, execute, or escalate)

- **Rate and impact limits**
  Even correct actions can be dangerous if executed too frequently or at scale. Guardrails should cap:
  - Number of actions per time window
  - Magnitude of changes (e.g., resource reallocation limits)
  - Concurrent interventions

For example, an AI agent optimizing batch workloads might be allowed to reorder jobs within a predefined group but prohibited from delaying regulatory or settlement workloads under any circumstance.

Escalation and Override Mechanisms

No AI agent should operate without a clear path to human intervention. Escalation and override mechanisms ensure that when uncertainty or risk increases, control automatically shifts back to human operators.

Key design elements include:

- **Confidence-based escalation**
  When an agent's confidence score falls below a defined threshold, it should:
  - Pause execution
  - Notify operators
  - Provide context and rationale for its recommendation
- **Human-in-the-loop checkpoints**
  High-impact actions—such as workload suspension or priority inversion—should require explicit human approval, especially during early stages of deployment.
- **Immediate override capability**
  Operators must be able to:
  - Disable an agent instantly

  - Revert its last actions
  - Switch to manual control without system disruption

A practical example:

During a peak processing window, an AI agent detects abnormal I/O contention and recommends reallocating resources. Because the action exceeds a predefined impact threshold, the agent escalates to the operator with a clear explanation and waits for approval before proceeding.

Testing Agent Decisions in Production-Like Environments

One of the most common mistakes in AI deployment is validating agents only in simplified or synthetic test environments. Safe autonomy requires rigorous testing that mirrors real operational complexity.

Best practices for testing include:

- **Shadow mode deployment**
  Agents run in parallel with production systems, making decisions but not executing them. This allows teams to:
  - Compare agent recommendations with human actions
  - Identify false positives and blind spots
  - Build confidence without risk
- **Replay and simulation testing**
  Historical system events are replayed to evaluate how an agent would have behaved under real conditions, including incidents and edge cases.
- **Progressive autonomy testing**
  Autonomy is increased gradually:
  - Observe → advise → execute low-risk actions → execute higher-impact actions

In a real-world setting, organizations often keep agents in shadow mode for weeks or months, using performance metrics and operator feedback to fine-tune behavior before enabling execution.

When to Roll Back Autonomy

Rolling back autonomy is not a failure—it is a sign of mature governance. Safe AI design assumes that conditions change, models drift, and operational realities evolve.

Organizations should roll back autonomy when:

- **Behavior deviates from expected outcomes**
  If an agent's actions consistently conflict with operational goals or human judgment, autonomy should be reduced.
- **Environmental changes occur**
  Major system upgrades, workload shifts, or regulatory changes may invalidate prior assumptions.
- **Trust erodes among operators**
  If operators begin to ignore or distrust agent recommendations, it signals a need to reassess autonomy levels.

Rollback mechanisms should be:

- Fast
- Reversible
- Well-documented
- Practiced through drills, just like incident response procedures

For example, during a major application migration, an organization may temporarily revert AI agents to advisory-only mode until system behavior stabilizes.

Designing Autonomy as a Journey

Safe agent autonomy is not a binary choice—it is a **continuous journey of calibration**. The most successful organizations treat autonomy as something that evolves alongside trust, governance maturity, and operational insight.

By combining strong guardrails, human-centric escalation, realistic testing, and deliberate rollback strategies, Agentic AI can operate with confidence in even the most demanding mainframe environments.

With this chapter, we complete the foundation for designing, governing, and scaling Agentic AI responsibly—setting the stage for organizations to modernize their mainframes not just with intelligence, but with wisdom.

Part IX: Implementation Playbooks and Tools

Up to this point in the book, we have focused on *why* Agentic AI matters for mainframes, *what* it looks like in practice, and *how* leaders and teams can safely plan, govern, and adopt it. In this part, we shift decisively from strategy to execution.

Part IX is about **turning intent into action.**

Mainframe teams often struggle not because they lack vision, but because they lack *practical, repeatable guidance.* Implementation efforts stall when every initiative feels like a one-off experiment, dependent on a few experts or undocumented tribal knowledge. This section addresses that gap by introducing structured playbooks and concrete tooling approaches that make Agentic AI implementation predictable, auditable, and scalable.

Rather than prescribing a single "right" architecture or vendor stack, this part emphasizes **patterns, decision frameworks, and integration strategies** that can be adapted to different enterprise realities—whether you are operating in a highly regulated financial institution, a government environment, or a hybrid cloud enterprise with decades of mainframe investment.

What This Part Covers

In this part, you will explore:

- How to move from pilot projects to repeatable implementations
- How to standardize Agentic AI deployments without stifling innovation
- How to select and integrate tools that complement—not disrupt—existing mainframe operations
- How to balance modern AI platforms with the reliability and discipline of traditional systems

Chapter 18: Agentic AI Implementation Playbooks

This chapter introduces **implementation playbooks**—step-by-step guides that help teams design, deploy, test, and operate agentic workflows on mainframes. You will learn how to structure playbooks for common use cases such as incident response, performance optimization, and operational forecasting, while embedding governance, safety controls, and rollback mechanisms from day one.

The focus is on repeatability: ensuring that successful implementations can be replicated across teams, systems, and environments without reinventing the wheel each time.

Chapter 19: Tools, Platforms, and Integration Options

No AI initiative succeeds without the right tooling ecosystem. This chapter explores the **tools and platforms** that enable Agentic AI in mainframe contexts, including data pipelines, orchestration layers, observability tools, and AI platforms. It also examines integration strategies that allow AI agents to work seamlessly across mainframe, distributed, and cloud environments—without creating new silos or operational risk.

Together, these chapters provide the practical foundation needed to move from concepts to production-ready Agentic AI solutions—closing the gap between strategy and sustained execution.

Part IX is where Agentic AI stops being theoretical and becomes operational.

Chapter 18: Agentic AI Implementation Playbooks

Agentic AI delivers the most value when it is implemented consistently, safely, and repeatably. In complex mainframe environments, success depends less on experimenting with isolated AI capabilities and more on establishing **clear playbooks** that teams can follow, adapt, and improve over time.

An implementation playbook is not a rigid script. Instead, it is a **practical guide** that defines intent, boundaries, roles, data flows, and decision points for a specific class of problems. Playbooks allow organizations to scale AI adoption without scaling risk—and to transfer knowledge across teams without relying on tribal expertise.

This chapter introduces four foundational playbooks that have proven effective across industries. While each targets a different operational challenge, they share common principles: human oversight, auditable decisions, incremental autonomy, and clear rollback paths.

Incident Management Playbook

Incident response is often the most compelling entry point for Agentic AI because it is data-rich, repetitive, and time-sensitive. In traditional environments, incident handling relies heavily on human intuition, manual log analysis, and escalation chains that can delay resolution.

An Agentic AI–driven incident management playbook typically follows this flow:

1. **Observe and Detect**
   The agent continuously monitors signals such as SMF records, system logs, alerts, and performance thresholds. Its role at this stage is observational—detecting anomalies,

correlations, or deviations from known baselines.

2. **Analyze and Recommend**
   When an incident is detected, the agent analyzes historical patterns and similar past events. Instead of acting immediately, it produces ranked recommendations: likely root causes, impacted systems, and suggested remediation steps.
3. **Human Validation**
   Operators review the agent's recommendations. In early implementations, humans remain firmly in control, using AI insights to accelerate diagnosis rather than replace judgment.
4. **Controlled Execution (Optional)**
   As trust matures, limited autonomous actions may be permitted—such as restarting non-critical services, adjusting thresholds, or opening incident tickets with pre-filled context.

Key Design Principle:

Never allow full autonomy at the start. Incident playbooks should evolve gradually from advisory to semi-autonomous, with strict guardrails and clear escalation paths.

Capacity Planning Playbook

Capacity planning on mainframes has traditionally been periodic, spreadsheet-driven, and reactive. Agentic AI enables a shift toward **continuous, predictive capacity management**.

A capacity planning playbook typically includes:

- **Data Aggregation**
  The agent ingests historical and real-time utilization data (CPU, memory, I/O, workload classes) from RMF and related sources.
- **Trend and Pattern Analysis**

Instead of static forecasts, the agent identifies seasonal patterns, workload growth trends, and abnormal consumption behaviors.

- **Scenario Simulation**
  The agent models "what-if" scenarios—such as onboarding new applications, shifting batch windows, or peak transaction spikes—and estimates capacity impact.
- **Recommendation and Reporting**
  Outputs are presented as clear recommendations: when to add capacity, rebalance workloads, or renegotiate software licensing tiers.

Key Design Principle:

Capacity agents should inform decisions, not automatically provision resources. The goal is better planning and negotiation leverage—not uncontrolled scaling.

Knowledge Augmentation Playbook

One of the most overlooked challenges in mainframe environments is **knowledge concentration**. Critical operational understanding often resides in a small number of experienced individuals, creating risk and bottlenecks.

The knowledge augmentation playbook focuses on capturing, organizing, and surfacing expertise through AI agents:

- **Knowledge Ingestion**
  The agent is trained on operational manuals, runbooks, historical incident tickets, and system documentation.
- **Contextual Assistance**
  When operators investigate an issue, the agent provides context-aware guidance—explaining log entries, suggesting diagnostic steps, or recalling similar past issues.
- **Learning from Interaction**

Each human interaction becomes feedback. Corrections, confirmations, and decisions refine the agent's understanding over time.

Key Design Principle:

The agent augments human capability—it does not replace expertise. Its success is measured by faster onboarding, reduced dependency on single experts, and improved confidence during operations.

Operational Optimization Playbook

Operational optimization playbooks target efficiency, stability, and consistency across day-to-day activities. These playbooks often combine insights from multiple agents.

Common use cases include:

- Optimizing batch schedules to reduce contention
- Identifying inefficient workload classifications
- Recommending parameter tuning for recurring performance issues
- Highlighting underutilized resources

The typical workflow involves:

1. **Baseline Definition** – Establish what "normal" and "good" look like.
2. **Continuous Evaluation** – Agents compare current behavior against baselines.
3. **Improvement Suggestions** – Recommendations are prioritized by impact and risk.
4. **Human Approval and Rollout** – Changes are reviewed, scheduled, and implemented through standard change management processes.

Key Design Principle:

Optimization should be continuous but conservative. Small, incremental improvements compound over time without destabilizing production systems.

Bringing Playbooks Together

While each playbook serves a distinct purpose, organizations gain the most value when they **standardize the structure** across all playbooks:

- Clear objectives and success metrics
- Defined autonomy levels
- Explicit human decision points
- Built-in auditability and logging
- Safe rollback mechanisms

By treating Agentic AI implementations as playbooks rather than experiments, enterprises can scale modernization efforts with confidence, consistency, and control.

In the next chapter, we will explore the **tools, platforms, and integration options** that make these playbooks operational—bridging mainframe systems, AI platforms, and enterprise architectures into a cohesive whole.

Chapter 19: Tools, Platforms, and Integration Options

Implementing Agentic AI for mainframes is not primarily a tooling challenge—but the **right tools and platforms make the difference between controlled progress and operational chaos**. Unlike greenfield AI projects, mainframe environments demand solutions that respect stability, auditability, security, and long-established operational practices.

This chapter provides practical guidance on the tooling landscape, integration approaches, and evaluation criteria that matter most when bringing Agentic AI into mission-critical systems.

AI Platforms and Orchestration Tools

At the heart of any agentic implementation is an AI platform capable of **reasoning, orchestration, and controlled execution**. In a mainframe context, these platforms typically sit *adjacent* to the system—not embedded directly within it.

Key capabilities to look for include:

- **Agent orchestration**
  The ability to define, coordinate, and sequence multiple agents (observer, advisor, executor) rather than relying on a single monolithic model.
- **Workflow integration**
  Support for event-driven and goal-driven workflows, allowing agents to react to system signals or pursue defined objectives.
- **Human-in-the-loop controls**
  Native mechanisms for approvals, overrides, and escalation before actions are taken.
- **Explainability and traceability**

Every recommendation or action should be logged with context, rationale, and source data.

Orchestration layers—often built on workflow engines or policy-driven automation frameworks—are especially important. They act as the **control plane**, ensuring AI agents operate within defined boundaries.

Open-Source vs. Commercial Solutions

Organizations often face an early decision: open-source, commercial platforms, or a hybrid approach.

Open-source solutions offer:

- Transparency into how models and workflows behave
- Flexibility to customize for niche mainframe use cases
- Reduced vendor lock-in

However, they also require:

- Strong in-house expertise
- Additional effort for security hardening and compliance
- Clear ownership for ongoing maintenance

Commercial solutions typically provide:

- Enterprise-grade support and SLAs
- Built-in governance, security, and compliance features
- Faster time-to-value for initial use cases

The most successful organizations adopt a **hybrid strategy**—using commercial platforms for orchestration, governance, and support, while selectively integrating open-source components where flexibility or innovation is needed.

Integration with Existing Mainframe Tooling

Agentic AI should extend—not disrupt—established mainframe operations.

Effective integrations often include:

- **Monitoring and metrics tools**
  Agents consume data from SMF, RMF, and existing monitoring dashboards rather than duplicating telemetry pipelines.
- **ITSM and incident management systems**
  AI-generated insights flow directly into ticketing systems, change records, and problem management workflows.
- **Automation frameworks**
  Existing schedulers, job control systems, and automation tools remain the execution backbone, with AI acting as a decision layer above them.
- **Security and identity systems**
  Agents authenticate and operate under the same access control models as human operators.

This approach ensures AI becomes a **first-class participant** in operations—not an external experiment running in parallel.

Selection Criteria and Evaluation Checklists

When evaluating tools and platforms, technical sophistication alone is not enough. Use the following criteria to guide decisions:

Operational Fit

- Does the tool integrate with existing workflows and tools?
- Can it operate without requiring disruptive architectural changes?

Governance and Safety

- Are autonomy levels configurable?
- Is every decision auditable and explainable?
- Are rollback and override mechanisms built in?

Security and Compliance

- Does the platform support enterprise authentication and authorization?
- Can it meet regulatory and audit requirements?

Scalability and Longevity

- Can the solution support multiple agents and use cases over time?
- Is there a clear product roadmap and ecosystem?

People and Skills

- Can current teams operate and maintain the platform?
- Is training and documentation sufficient for mixed-skill environments?

Closing Perspective

Tools do not create successful Agentic AI implementations—**disciplined integration and thoughtful selection do**. The best platforms fade into the background, enabling teams to focus on outcomes rather than infrastructure.

As you move from experimentation to production, remember: the goal is not to find the most advanced AI tool, but the one that best supports **safe autonomy, operational trust, and long-term modernization**.

With the foundations, strategies, metrics, and playbooks now in place, you are equipped to turn Agentic AI from a concept into a sustainable capability—one that evolves alongside your mainframe environment rather than competing with it.

Part X: The Road Ahead

Modernizing the mainframe with Agentic AI is not a project with a finish line—it is a **long-term capability that evolves alongside the business, technology, and people who rely on it**. By the time organizations reach this stage, they have moved beyond experimentation and isolated wins. The question is no longer *"Can we do this?"* but *"How do we sustain it, scale it, and make it part of how we operate?"*

Part X looks forward. It shifts the focus from frameworks, tools, and case studies to **mindset, leadership, and personal accountability**. This final section is designed to help both organizations and individuals internalize modernization as an ongoing discipline rather than a one-time initiative.

Chapter 20: Building a Continuous Modernization Mindset explores how organizations avoid stagnation after early success. It examines how to institutionalize learning, adapt governance as autonomy grows, and continuously reassess what "modern" means in a rapidly changing AI landscape. You will see how leading organizations treat modernization as a cycle—observe, learn, adjust, and improve—rather than a linear roadmap that eventually expires.

Chapter 21: Your Personal Modernization Action Plan brings the journey down to the individual level. Whether you are a systems programmer, architect, operations leader, or executive sponsor, modernization ultimately advances through personal decisions and daily actions. This chapter helps you translate the concepts in this book into a clear, practical plan tailored to your role, influence, and organizational context.

Together, these chapters close the book not with conclusions, but with **direction**. They are intended to leave you confident, motivated, and prepared to lead or support Agentic AI–driven modernization long after the final page—because the road ahead is not about reaching a destination, but about **continuing to move forward with purpose and control**.

Chapter 20: Building a Continuous Modernization Mindset

Mainframe modernization with Agentic AI does not end when the first agents go live or when initial KPIs improve. In fact, that moment is where the *real* work begins. Organizations that succeed long term are the ones that shift their thinking—from modernization as a **project** to modernization as an **organizational capability**. This chapter explores how that mindset shift happens, how Agentic AI can scale safely over time, and how the role of the mainframe professional evolves in this new reality.

From Projects to Capabilities

Traditional modernization efforts are often framed as finite initiatives:

- A migration program
- A tooling upgrade
- A multi-year transformation roadmap

These approaches create momentum—but they also create an endpoint. Once the project closes, learning slows, ownership blurs, and systems gradually return to "business as usual."

A continuous modernization mindset treats AI-enabled modernization as a **living capability**, not a checklist.

What changes when modernization becomes a capability:

- Teams continuously identify new optimization opportunities
- AI agents are refined, retrained, or retired as conditions change
- Governance adapts as trust and maturity increase
- Learning is built into daily operations, not quarterly reviews

For example, instead of launching a one-time "AI incident response project," a mature organization builds a **standing incident intelligence capability**. Agents evolve as new failure patterns emerge, new applications are introduced, or workloads shift across hybrid environments.

The mainframe becomes not just stable—but *adaptable*.

Scaling Agentic AI Responsibly

Early AI wins are often tightly controlled:

- One or two agents
- Narrow scopes
- Heavy human oversight

Scaling too fast can erode trust, increase risk, and trigger resistance. Scaling too slowly, on the other hand, can stall momentum and limit value.

Responsible scaling is about **expanding autonomy without expanding uncertainty**.

Key principles for safe scaling include:

1. **Progressive Autonomy**
    - Start with observe → advise → execute models
    - Increase autonomy only after consistent, explainable performance
    - Document decision thresholds clearly
2. **Layered Safeguards**
    - Human override mechanisms
    - Policy-based constraints on agent actions
    - Automated rollback and alerting
3. **Capability-Based Expansion**
    - Scale by function (incident response, capacity planning, compliance)
    - Not by raw number of agents

- Ensure each capability has clear ownership

A practical example: an agent that initially only recommends batch rescheduling during peak windows may, over time, be trusted to execute changes automatically—but only within predefined boundaries and during approved timeframes.

Scaling succeeds when **control scales alongside intelligence**.

Preparing for Future AI Advances

Agentic AI will not stand still. Models will improve, reasoning will deepen, and integration patterns will change. Organizations that lock themselves into today's assumptions risk tomorrow's disruption.

A future-ready modernization mindset focuses on **adaptability, not prediction**.

To prepare for what's next:

- **Design for Replaceability**
  - Treat AI models as components, not foundations
  - Avoid hard-coding logic into proprietary black boxes
- **Invest in Data Readiness**
  - High-quality operational data outlives any single AI model
  - Clean logs, metrics, and event streams remain reusable assets
- **Continuously Revisit Governance**
  - What required human approval last year may not need it next year
  - New regulations or risks may introduce new controls

Rather than asking, *"What will AI look like in five years?"*, leading teams ask:

"How quickly can we adapt when it changes?"

The Evolving Role of the Mainframe Professional

Perhaps the most profound change in continuous modernization is not technological—it is human.

The mainframe professional is no longer defined solely by:

- Deep system commands
- Manual troubleshooting
- Reactive operations

Instead, their role expands into new dimensions:

- **System Steward** – defining guardrails, policies, and trust boundaries
- **AI Collaborator** – interpreting agent recommendations and refining behavior
- **Strategic Translator** – connecting operational insights to business outcomes
- **Change Leader** – helping teams adopt new workflows with confidence

This does not diminish traditional skills. It **amplifies them.** Deep system knowledge becomes more valuable when paired with AI that can act at scale—under human guidance.

In this model, professionals spend less time fighting fires and more time shaping how systems behave.

Key Takeaways

- Continuous modernization is a capability, not a one-time project
- Scaling Agentic AI requires deliberate increases in autonomy with strong safeguards

- Future readiness comes from adaptable architecture and strong data foundations
- The mainframe professional evolves into a steward, collaborator, and modernization leader

---

In the next chapter, we turn this organizational mindset into **personal action**.

Chapter 21: Your Personal Modernization Action Plan will help you translate everything you've learned into concrete steps you can take—starting now—to lead, influence, or support Agentic AI–driven modernization in your own environment.

Chapter 21: Your Personal Modernization Action Plan

Modernization does not start with tools, budgets, or executive mandates—it starts with **individual action**. Whether you are a systems programmer, architect, operations leader, or technology manager, your ability to translate knowledge into practice determines whether Agentic AI becomes a real capability or just another strategic conversation.

This final chapter is designed to help you move from understanding to **execution**. You will assess where you are today, define what you can realistically accomplish in the next 90 days, and position yourself as a credible, trusted leader in AI-driven mainframe modernization—regardless of your formal job title.

Self-Assessment Checklist

Before you plan your next steps, you need a clear view of your current position. Use the checklist below as an honest reflection—not a test.

Ask yourself:

Technical Understanding

- Do I clearly understand what Agentic AI is—and what it is not?
- Can I explain agent roles (observer, advisor, executor) in simple terms?
- Do I know which mainframe data sources (SMF, RMF, logs) are most valuable for AI use cases?

Operational Readiness

- Can I identify at least two operational pain points that AI could realistically help address?

- Do I understand current incident, capacity, or compliance workflows well enough to augment them?
- Do I know where automation has failed or stalled in the past—and why?

Organizational Awareness

- Who are the key stakeholders that influence modernization decisions?
- What are the main concerns around risk, compliance, or job security?
- How open is my organization to experimentation versus control?

Personal Influence

- Am I seen as a problem solver or a "tool expert" only?
- Can I communicate technical ideas in business language?
- Do people trust my judgment when systems are under pressure?

Any "no" answers are not weaknesses—they are **starting points.**

Your 30–60–90 Day Action Plan

A personal modernization journey succeeds when it is incremental, visible, and aligned with real work.

First 30 Days: Observe and Frame

Focus on learning and context.

- Identify one operational area wherc decisions are frequent and repetitive
- Map the current workflow from signal to action
- Document where humans hesitate, double-check, or escalate
- Begin framing AI as *decision support*, not replacement

Your goal is clarity—not implementation.

Next 60 Days: Pilot and Influence

Shift from observation to experimentation.

- Propose a narrow, low-risk AI-assisted use case
- Start with "observe and advise" agents
- Involve operators early and solicit feedback
- Track outcomes using operational metrics, not hype

At this stage, credibility matters more than sophistication.

By 90 Days: Demonstrate and Expand

Turn learning into momentum.

- Present measurable results to stakeholders
- Show how AI reduced noise, improved response time, or increased confidence
- Recommend next steps with clear guardrails
- Position modernization as a capability, not a one-off success

By now, you should be known as someone who *delivers*, not just someone who talks about AI.

Building Internal Credibility as an AI Modernization Leader

You do not need a formal leadership title to lead modernization.

Credibility is built when you:

- Respect operational realities
- Acknowledge risks openly
- Protect system stability
- Translate complexity into confidence

Avoid positioning yourself as "the AI expert." Instead, become the person who **connects AI to real operational outcomes.**

Practical ways to build trust include:

- Sharing failures and lessons learned
- Inviting skeptics into pilots
- Using plain language instead of buzzwords
- Emphasizing safety, auditability, and control

The fastest way to lose credibility is to oversell AI.

The fastest way to gain it is to make life easier for the people running the system.

Continuing Education and Next Learning Paths

Agentic AI and mainframe modernization will continue to evolve. Staying effective means committing to **lifelong learning**.

Recommended next steps include:

- Deepening skills in AI governance and explainability
- Learning hybrid cloud integration patterns
- Exploring industry-specific modernization case studies
- Practicing change leadership and stakeholder communication

Look for advanced courses, workshops, and certifications focused on:

- AI in regulated environments
- Enterprise architecture and systems thinking
- Modern mainframe tooling and observability platforms

Most importantly, stay curious. The professionals who thrive are those who keep learning while staying grounded in operational reality.

Final Reflection

Modernization is no longer about leaving the mainframe behind.

It is about **making it smarter, safer, and more adaptive**.

With the knowledge from this course—and the action plan you now have—you are equipped to:

- Lead responsibly
- Influence confidently
- And modernize continuously

Your journey in Agentic AI for Mainframes does not end here. This is where it truly begins.

Epilogue: From Legacy to Leadership

For decades, the mainframe has been described using the language of the past—*legacy, old, rigid, expensive.* Yet throughout this book and the course that accompanies it, a different truth has emerged: the mainframe has endured not despite change, but **because it adapts to it**.

What is changing now is not the relevance of the mainframe, but the **expectations placed upon it**.

Enterprises no longer ask only for stability and throughput. They ask for insight, agility, resilience, and speed—without compromising trust. Agentic AI represents a powerful response to those expectations, not by replacing human expertise, but by amplifying it. When thoughtfully designed, governed, and adopted, agentic systems become partners in decision-making, quietly strengthening the systems that power the world's most critical institutions.

This is why modernization today is less about technology and more about **leadership**.

The leaders of this next era are not defined by job titles or years of service. They are defined by mindset. They are professionals who respect the past while actively shaping the future. They understand that innovation does not mean recklessness, and that safety does not mean stagnation. They recognize that trust—between humans, systems, and AI—must be earned continuously.

As you step forward from this book, remember:

- Modernization is not a single project; it is a sustained capability.
- AI is not a shortcut; it is a responsibility.
- The mainframe is not a barrier; it is a foundation.

You now carry a rare and valuable perspective—one that bridges mission-critical systems, modern AI capabilities, and human-centered leadership. Use it thoughtfully. Use it boldly. And above all, use it to make systems not just more efficient, but more **reliable, explainable, and humane**.

The story of mainframe modernization is still being written.

And now, you are part of the authorship.

Appendix A: Glossary of Agentic AI and Mainframe Terms

This glossary provides clear, practical definitions of key terms used throughout this book and the accompanying course. The intent is not academic completeness, but operational clarity—helping you quickly align concepts across AI, mainframes, and modernization initiatives.

A

Agent (AI Agent)

A software entity that can perceive system events, reason about goals or policies, and take actions autonomously or semi-autonomously. In a mainframe context, agents often observe operational signals, recommend actions, or execute predefined workflows.

Agentic AI

A class of AI systems designed to act with purpose, autonomy, and context-awareness, rather than merely responding to prompts. Agentic AI systems can plan, decide, act, and learn within defined boundaries.

Autonomy Level

The degree of independence granted to an AI agent, ranging from advisory-only (human approval required) to fully autonomous execution within strict guardrails.

API (Application Programming Interface)

A standardized interface that allows systems—mainframe or distributed—to communicate and exchange data or services.

B

Batch Processing

A processing mode where jobs are executed without user interaction, commonly used in mainframe environments for high-volume, scheduled workloads.

Behavioral Guardrails

Rules, constraints, and policies that limit what an AI agent can do, ensuring safety, compliance, and predictability.

C

Change Management

Structured approaches to transitioning individuals and teams from current workflows to AI-enabled processes, focusing on adoption, trust, and skill development.

COBOL

A high-level programming language widely used on mainframes for business-critical applications, especially in banking, insurance, and government systems.

Compliance-by-Design

An approach where regulatory, audit, and security requirements are embedded into AI systems from the outset rather than added later.

D

Decision Boundary

A predefined limit that determines when an AI agent can act independently and when human intervention is required.

Distributed Systems

Computing environments that span multiple servers or platforms, often integrated with mainframes through APIs or messaging layers.

E

Event-Driven Architecture

A system design where actions are triggered by events (such as alerts, thresholds, or failures) rather than continuous polling.

Explainability (AI Explainability)

The ability to understand and trace why an AI system made a particular recommendation or decision—critical in regulated mainframe environments.

F

Feedback Loop

A continuous mechanism where human input, system outcomes, and performance metrics are fed back into AI models or agents to improve future behavior.

Fail-Safe Mechanism

Controls that ensure systems revert to a safe state if an AI agent behaves unexpectedly or encounters uncertainty.

G

Governance Framework

A structured set of policies, roles, and processes that define how AI systems are approved, monitored, and controlled.

H

Human-in-the-Loop (HITL)

A model where AI agents provide recommendations, but humans make final decisions and approvals.

Human-on-the-Loop (HOTL)

A supervisory model where AI agents act autonomously, but humans monitor outcomes and intervene only when needed.

I

Incident Management

Processes for detecting, diagnosing, and resolving system incidents—an early and common use case for agentic AI in mainframes.

Interoperability

The ability of mainframe systems to integrate seamlessly with cloud, distributed, and AI platforms.

K

Knowledge Augmentation

Using AI to enhance human expertise by surfacing insights, documentation, historical patterns, or recommendations in real time.

L

Lagging Indicator

A metric that reflects outcomes after an event has occurred (e.g., downtime duration).

Leading Indicator

A predictive metric that signals potential issues before they happen (e.g., resource saturation trends).

M

Mainframe Modernization

The strategic evolution of mainframe systems to improve agility, integration, and value—without necessarily replacing core platforms.

MTTR (Mean Time to Repair)

A key operational metric measuring the average time required to resolve system incidents.

O

Observability

The ability to understand system behavior through logs, metrics, and traces—foundational for agentic AI decision-making.

Operational Data

Runtime data generated by systems, including logs, performance metrics, and alerts.

P

Phased Autonomy

A strategy of gradually increasing AI agent independence as trust, accuracy, and governance mature.

Playbook (Operational Playbook)

A predefined set of actions and decision rules that guide AI agents during specific scenarios.

R

RMF (Resource Measurement Facility)

IBM mainframe component providing detailed performance and resource usage data.

Rollback Mechanism

A capability to reverse AI-driven changes or decisions when risks or errors are detected.

S

SMF (System Management Facilities)

A core mainframe feature that collects detailed system, workload, and accounting data.

SYSLOG

System logs capturing operational messages, errors, and events.

Scope Control

The practice of limiting AI initiatives to clearly defined boundaries to reduce risk.

T

Trust Calibration

The process of aligning human trust with actual AI system performance—neither over-trusting nor under-utilizing AI agents.

U

Use Case Prioritization

The structured selection of AI initiatives based on value, feasibility, and risk.

W

Workflow Orchestration

Coordinating multiple automated steps, systems, or agents into a cohesive operational process.

Z

z/OS

IBM's flagship mainframe operating system, widely used in enterprise environments.

This glossary is designed to be a living reference. As agentic AI and mainframe technologies evolve, so too will the language used to describe them—but the principles behind these terms will continue to anchor safe, effective modernization.

Appendix B: Sample Modernization Templates and Worksheets

This appendix provides practical, ready-to-use templates and worksheets that support the planning, execution, and governance of agentic AI–driven mainframe modernization initiatives. These tools are designed to be simple, adaptable, and immediately useful—whether you are launching a pilot program or scaling AI across the enterprise.

Each template can be printed, shared digitally, or adapted into your organization's preferred documentation or governance tools.

Template 1: Mainframe Modernization Readiness Assessment

Purpose:

To evaluate organizational, technical, and cultural readiness before introducing agentic AI.

Instructions:

Rate each item on a scale of 1 (Not Ready) to 5 (Fully Ready).

Area	**Assessment Question**	**Score (1–5)**
Strategy	Modernization goals are clearly tied to business outcomes	
Leadership	Executive sponsorship is identified and active	
Data	Operational data (SMF, RMF, logs) is accessible and reliable	
Governance	AI governance and risk controls are defined	
Culture	Teams are open to AI-assisted decision-making	
Skills	Staff has baseline AI and automation knowledge	

Interpretation:

- **30–35:** Strong readiness
- **20–29:** Proceed with targeted improvements

- **Below 20:** Address foundational gaps first

Template 2: AI Use Case Definition Worksheet

Purpose:

To clearly define and prioritize AI modernization opportunities.

Use Case Name:

Operational Area: (e.g., Incident Management, Capacity Planning)

Problem Statement:

What recurring operational issue are we trying to solve?

Current Process Pain Points:

-
-

Proposed AI Role:

☐ Observer ☐ Advisor ☐ Executor ☐ Coordinator

Expected Benefits:

- Reduced MTTR
- Improved availability
- Lower operational risk
- Productivity gains

Risk Level:

☐ Low ☐ Medium ☐ High

Success Metrics:

-

Template 3: Stakeholder Mapping Worksheet

Purpose:

To identify who must be involved, informed, or accountable.

Stakeholder Group	Role	Concerns	Level of Influence
Executive Sponsor			High
IT Operations			
Security & Compliance			
Business Owners			
AI / Data Team			

Tip:

Pay special attention to stakeholders with high influence and high risk sensitivity.

Template 4: Agent Autonomy Design Checklist

Purpose:

To safely define how much control an AI agent is allowed.

☐ Agent actions are clearly documented
☐ Decision boundaries are defined
☐ Human approval points are identified
☐ Rollback and override mechanisms exist
☐ Logging and audit trails are enabled
☐ Escalation paths are documented

Approved Autonomy Level:

☐ Advisory only
☐ Conditional execution
☐ Fully autonomous (within guardrails)

Template 5: AI Governance and Risk Review

Purpose:

To ensure compliance, auditability, and operational safety.

Governance Questions:

- Is the AI model explainable to auditors?
- Are data sources approved and secured?
- Are decisions traceable and logged?
- Has legal/compliance reviewed the use case?

Approval Status:
☐ Approved ☐ Approved with Conditions ☐ Not Approved
Conditions or Mitigations Required:

-

Template 6: Metrics and ROI Tracking Worksheet
Purpose:
To track value over time and communicate results.
Baseline Metrics (Before AI):

- MTTR:
- Incident Volume:
- System Availability:

Post-Implementation Metrics:

- MTTR:
- Incident Volume:
- System Availability:

Qualitative Benefits:

- Improved confidence in operations
- Faster decision-making
- Reduced staff burnout

Reporting Frequency:
☐ Weekly ☐ Monthly ☐ Quarterly

Template 7: 30–60–90 Day Modernization Action Plan
Purpose:
To translate learning into action.
First 30 Days (Assess & Align):

- Identify 1–2 AI use cases
- Secure executive sponsorship
- Assess data readiness

Next 60 Days (Pilot & Learn):

- Implement limited-scope agent
- Monitor results and risks
- Gather team feedback

Next 90 Days (Refine & Scale):

- Adjust autonomy levels
- Expand to adjacent workflows
- Prepare management reporting

Template 8: Lessons Learned and Feedback Loop

Purpose:

To institutionalize learning and continuous improvement.

What Worked Well:

What Didn't Work:

Unexpected Outcomes:

Changes for Next Iteration:

How to Use These Templates

These templates are most effective when used together—not as paperwork, but as living tools. Revisit them regularly, update them as AI maturity grows, and encourage teams to treat modernization as a continuous capability rather than a one-time project.

Used consistently, these worksheets will help you turn agentic AI concepts into disciplined, trusted, and scalable modernization outcomes.

Appendix C: Executive Briefing Templates

Modernizing mainframe environments with Agentic AI requires more than technical excellence—it requires **clear, credible communication with executive leadership**. Executives care about outcomes, risk, alignment, and confidence. This appendix provides ready-to-use briefing templates that help translate complex AI and modernization initiatives into language that resonates with senior stakeholders.

These templates are intentionally concise, outcome-focused, and adaptable. They can be used in board briefings, CIO updates, steering committee meetings, or funding approval discussions.

Template 1: Executive One-Page Modernization Overview

Purpose:

Provide a high-level snapshot of the modernization initiative in under five minutes.

Recommended Use:

Initial executive briefings, quarterly updates, or decision checkpoints.

Structure:

1. Initiative Summary (3–4 sentences)

- What problem are we solving?
- Why does it matter now?
- Why is Agentic AI part of the solution?

Example:

"This initiative introduces Agentic AI into our mainframe operations to reduce incident resolution time, improve system resilience, and support continuous modernization without disrupting mission-critical workloads."

2. Business Outcomes (Bullet Points)

- Reduced operational risk
- Improved service availability
- Faster decision-making
- Better utilization of skilled staff

3. Scope at a Glance

- Systems involved
- Processes affected
- Level of AI autonomy (advisory, semi-autonomous, supervised)

4. Risk & Governance Snapshot

- Human oversight model
- Compliance alignment
- Fail-safe mechanisms

5. Status / Decision Required

- Current phase (pilot, rollout, optimization)
- Executive support or decision needed (if any)

Template 2: AI Value and ROI Briefing

Purpose:

Demonstrate measurable value beyond technical metrics.

Recommended Use:

Funding approvals, budget reviews, or post-pilot evaluations.

Structure:

1. Value Hypothesis

- What value did we expect to create?
- What assumptions were made?

2. Measured Outcomes

- Operational metrics (e.g., MTTR reduction, fewer manual interventions)
- Financial indicators (cost avoidance, productivity gains)
- Risk metrics (incident frequency, compliance findings)

3. Qualitative Benefits

- Staff confidence and workload balance
- Knowledge retention and decision consistency
- Improved audit readiness

4. ROI Narrative (Not Just Numbers)

- "Before vs. After" story
- What changed in daily operations
- Why this scales well

5. Next Value Milestone

- What is the next achievable improvement?
- What additional investment enables it?

Template 3: Risk, Compliance, and Governance Briefing
Purpose:
Build executive confidence that AI is being deployed responsibly.
Recommended Use:
Risk committees, audit discussions, regulated environments.
Structure:
1. Governance Model Overview

- Who owns decisions?

- Who approves changes?
- Who can override AI actions?

2. AI Control Points

- Human-in-the-loop checkpoints
- Escalation paths
- Rollback procedures

3. Compliance Alignment

- Regulatory frameworks considered
- Audit trails and explainability
- Data access and privacy controls

4. Risk Reduction Achieved

- Reduced human error
- Faster detection of anomalies
- Improved consistency in response

5. Open Risks & Mitigations

- Known limitations
- Planned safeguards
- Continuous monitoring approach

Template 4: Scaling and Roadmap Briefing

Purpose:

Show how the initiative evolves from pilot to enterprise capability.

Recommended Use:

Strategic planning sessions, roadmap approvals.

Structure:

1. Current State

- What is working today?
- What has been validated?

2. Near-Term Expansion (Next 6–12 Months)

- Additional use cases
- Broader system coverage
- Increased autonomy (if appropriate)

3. Long-Term Vision

- From project to platform
- Integration with enterprise AI strategy
- Organizational capability building

4. Investment vs. Return Outlook

- Incremental costs
- Expected cumulative benefits

5. Executive Enablement Needed

- Policy support
- Cross-team alignment
- Sponsorship for change adoption

Template 5: Executive Q&A Preparation Sheet
Purpose:
Prepare modernization leaders for predictable executive questions.
Common Executive Questions to Prepare For:

- "What happens if the AI gets it wrong?"

- "How do we maintain control?"
- "How does this compare to replacing the system?"
- "What skills do our people need now?"
- "How do we stop this from becoming shelfware?"

Recommended Approach:
Answer in **business terms first**, then offer technical detail only if requested.

Final Guidance for Using These Templates

- Keep slides minimal—**the story matters more than the diagram**
- Anchor every discussion in **risk, value, and confidence**
- Avoid AI jargon unless it directly supports a business outcome
- Position Agentic AI as a **capability**, not a one-time project

Used consistently, these executive briefing templates help ensure that Agentic AI for Mainframes is understood, supported, and sustained at the leadership level—where modernization success is ultimately decided.

Appendix D: Further Reading and Learning Resources

Modernizing mainframe environments with Agentic AI is a multidisciplinary journey that spans systems engineering, AI, governance, leadership, and change management. This appendix provides a curated list of **trusted, real-world resources** to help you deepen your understanding, validate decisions, and continue learning well beyond this course.

The resources are grouped by theme so you can quickly find what is most relevant to your current role or challenge.

---

1. Mainframe Modernization and Enterprise Systems

Books

- **"Mainframe Modernization Handbook"** – Modern Systems (various editions)
  A practical overview of modernization strategies, risks, and patterns used by large enterprises.
- **"Enterprise IT Architecture for Digital Business"** by Charles T. Betz
  Useful for understanding how mainframes fit into modern digital and hybrid architectures.

IBM Resources

- **IBM Z Documentation and Redbooks**
  Especially relevant titles include:
    - *IBM Z and Cloud Modernization*
    - *Modernizing Applications on IBM Z*
      IBM Redbooks are authoritative, free, and widely used by enterprise architects.

- **IBM Z Digital Badge Program**
  Offers structured learning paths on z/OS, hybrid cloud, and AI integration.

---

2. AI, Automation, and Agent-Based Systems
Books

- **"Artificial Intelligence: A Modern Approach"** by Stuart Russell and Peter Norvig
  A foundational reference for understanding AI concepts, including agents and decision-making.
- **"Designing Autonomous AI"** by D. Woods and others (academic/industry publications)
  Focuses on safe autonomy and human oversight in complex systems.

Research and Thought Leadership

- **MIT CSAIL publications on AI systems and autonomy**
- **Stanford AI Index Report**
  Provides annual insights into AI capabilities, risks, and adoption trends.

Online Platforms

- **Coursera / edX** courses from institutions such as Stanford, MIT, and IBM on:
  - AI systems design
  - Machine learning operations (MLOps)
  - Responsible AI

---

3. Governance, Risk, and Compliance
Standards and Frameworks

- **ISACA COBIT® 2019 / COBIT® 2023**
  Widely used for IT governance and control, including emerging technology oversight.
- **NIST AI Risk Management Framework (AI RMF)**
  A practical framework for managing AI risks in regulated environments.
- **ISO/IEC 23894:2023 (AI Risk Management)**
  An emerging international standard for AI risk governance.

Professional Bodies

- **ISACA** – Research papers and guidance on AI governance and auditability
- **IEEE Standards Association** – Ethical and governance standards for AI systems

---

4. Hybrid Cloud, Integration, and Architecture Books

- **"Building Microservices"** by Sam Newman
  Helpful for understanding service exposure and interoperability with mainframes.
- **"Cloud Native Transformation"** by Pini Reznik, Jamie Dobson, and Michelle Gienow
  Relevant for organizations integrating legacy systems into cloud-native strategies.

Architecture Frameworks

- **TOGAF® Standard (The Open Group)**
  Commonly used for enterprise architecture planning involving legacy and modern platforms.

5. Change Management and Leadership
Books

- **"Leading Change"** by John P. Kotter
  A classic reference for driving adoption in large, risk-averse organizations.
- **"The Phoenix Project"** by Gene Kim, Kevin Behr, and George Spafford
  While fictional, it is widely used to explain operational change and cultural transformation.
- **"Team Topologies"** by Matthew Skelton and Manuel Pais
  Useful for redefining team structures in AI-enabled operations.

---

6. Metrics, ROI, and Executive Communication
Books

- **"Measuring and Managing Performance in Organizations"** by Robert D. Austin
  A foundational text on choosing metrics that drive the right behaviors.
- **"Storytelling with Data"** by Cole Nussbaumer Knaflic
  Highly practical for presenting technical results to executive audiences.

Industry Resources

- **Gartner Research (IT Operations, AIOps, and Modernization)**
  Often referenced by executives for decision-making context.
- **McKinsey & Company AI and Digital Transformation Insights**

Provides business-focused perspectives on AI value realization.

---

7. Continuing Education and Professional Development

Certifications and Programs

- **IBM Certified Specialist – IBM Z**
- **ISACA Certifications** (CISA, CISM, CRISC) for governance-focused professionals
- **Linux Foundation Training** on cloud, DevOps, and systems reliability

Communities

- **SHARE Association (Mainframe Community)**
- **Open Mainframe Project (Linux Foundation)**
- **LinkedIn Groups and Forums focused on IBM Z and Enterprise AI**

Closing Note

No single book, framework, or course will provide all the answers for mainframe modernization with Agentic AI. The most effective professionals combine **foundational knowledge, real-world experimentation, and continuous learning**.

Use this appendix as a living reference. Revisit it as your role evolves—from learner, to implementer, to leader—and as Agentic AI continues to reshape how mission-critical systems are designed, operated, and governed.

Don't miss out!

Visit the website below and you can sign up to receive emails whenever Ricardo Nuqui publishes a new book. There's no charge and no obligation.

https://books2read.com/r/B-A-NBRMC-DYQVI

BOOKS 2 READ

Connecting independent readers to independent writers.

Did you love *Leading Mainframe Modernization with Agentic AI*? Then you should read *Future-Proof Your Mainframes with AI/ML*[1] by Ricardo Nuqui!

[2]

Future-Proof Your Mainframes with AI/ML Discover how to bring the power of Artificial Intelligence and Machine Learning to the heart of enterprise technology—your mainframes. This comprehensive guide equips IT leaders, systems managers, and enterprise architects with the knowledge and tools to modernize mainframe systems and unlock their full potential in today's AI-driven world.

From understanding foundational concepts of AI/ML to implementing cutting-edge solutions, this book bridges the gap between legacy systems and innovative technologies. Explore how predictive analytics, automation, and hybrid cloud architectures can

1. https://books2read.com/u/3R7D0p

2. https://books2read.com/u/3R7D0p

enhance performance, scalability, and security for mission-critical operations.

Inside, you'll find:

Step-by-step strategies for integrating AI/ML into mainframe environments.Tools and frameworks to streamline workflows and optimize performance.Real-world case studies showcasing successful AI/ML implementations.Practical insights on data preparation, model deployment, and continuous improvement.Best practices for ensuring compliance, security, and system stability.

Whether you're modernizing existing systems, enhancing data-driven decision-making, or future-proofing your infrastructure, *Future-Proof Your Mainframes with AI/ML* is the ultimate resource for driving innovation and sustaining competitive advantage in a rapidly evolving technological landscape.

Transform your mainframes. Elevate your enterprise. Redefine the future.

Also by Ricardo Nuqui

CyberSecurity

The CISSP Fast-Track: Conquer the 8 Domains

Mainframes

Mastering Mainframe Modernization
Mainframe Meets Modernization: Mastering Hybrid Cloud Design
Mainframe Mastery with DevOps: Integrating Legacy Systems with Agile Practices
Mainframe Modernization: CI/CD Mastery
Mainframe to Cloud Mastery: Best Practices
Mainframe Modernization with DevOps Mastery
Mainframe Containerization Mastery
Future-Proof Your Mainframes with AI/ML
Smart Architectures: AI/ML in Mainframe-Cloud Environments
Future-Proof z/OS: A Comprehensive Guide to Mainframe Modernization
Mastering USS Made Simple: A Practical Guide to Modernizing Your Mainframe Without Linux Expertise
The z/OS Modernization Handbook
Mainframe Assembler Programming: A Comprehensive Guide
Leading Mainframe Modernization with Agentic AI

www.ingramcontent.com/pod-product-compliance
Ingram Content Group UK Ltd.
Pitfield, Milton Keynes, MK11 3LW, UK
UKHW020123290926
15471UKWH00003B/256

9 798233 979316